JOHN BEVERE

THE FEAR OF THE LORD

DISCOVER THE KEY TO
INTIMATELY KNOWING GOD

Devotional Workbook

The Fear of the Lord Devotional Workbook
Copyright © 2010 by Messenger International

Published by: Messenger International, P.O. Box 888, Palmer Lake, CO 80133-0888
All rights reserved. No portion of this book may be reproduced, stored in a retrieval system, or transmitted in any form or by any means —electronic, mechanical, photocopy, recording, or any other—except for brief quotations in printed reviews, without the prior permission of the publisher.

Unless otherwise noted, Scripture quotations that are marked NKJV are taken from the NEW KING JAMES VERSION.
Copyright © 1979, 1980, 1982 by Thomas Nelson, Inc. Used by permission. All rights reserved.

Scripture quotations marked AMP are taken from the AMPLIFIED® Bible.
Copyright © 1954, 1958, 1962, 1964, 1965, 1987 by The Lockman Foundation. Used by permission. (www.Lockman.org)

Scripture quotations marked CEV are taken from the CONTEMPORARY ENGLISH VERSION®.
Copyright © 1995 by American Bible Society. All rights reserved.

Scripture quotations marked GW are taken from GOD'S WORD®, © 1995 God's Word to the Nations. Used by permission of Baker Publishing Group.

Scripture quotations marked KJV are from The Holy Bible, KING JAMES VERSION.
Copyright © 1970 by Thomas Nelson, Inc.

Scripture quotations marked NASB are taken from the NEW AMERICAN STANDARD BIBLE®.
Copyright © 1960, 1962, 1963, 1968, 1971, 1972, 1973, 1975, 1977, 1995 by The Lockman Foundation. Used by permission. (www.Lockman.org)

Scripture quotations marked NIV are taken from the HOLY BIBLE: NEW INTERNATIONAL VERSION®.
Copyright © 1973, 1978, 1984 by International Bible Society. Used by permission of Zondervan Publishing House. All rights reserved.

The "NIV" and "New International Version" trademarks are registered in the United States Patent and Trademark Office by International Bible Society. Use of either trademark requires the permission of International Bible Society.

Scripture quotations marked NLT are taken from the Holy Bible, NEW LIVING TRANSLATION.
Copyright © 1996, 2004.
Used by permission of Tyndale House Publishers, Inc., Wheaton, IL 60189. All rights reserved.
Note: Some New Living Translation (NLT) Scripture quotations are taken from the Second Edition.

Scripture quotations marked The Message are taken from THE MESSAGE.
Copyright © 1993, 1994, 1995, 1996, 2000, 2001, 2002. Used by permission of NavPress Publishing Group.

Scripture quotations marked TEV are from TODAY'S ENGLISH VERSION.
Copyright © by American Bible Society, 1966, 1971, 1976, 1992.

Scripture quotations marked TLB are taken from THE LIVING BIBLE.
Copyright © 1971 by Tyndale House Publishers, Wheaton, IL 60187. All rights reserved.

Unless otherwise noted, italics and bold treatment used in leader quotes indicate the author's added emphasis.

WRITTEN AND EDITED BY:
Vincent M. Newfield
New Fields & Company
P. O. Box 622 • Hillsboro, Missouri 63050
www.preparethewaytoday.org

COVER, DESIGN & PRINT PRODUCTION:
Eastco Multi Media Solutions, Inc.
3646 California Rd. • Orchard Park, NY 14127
www.eastcomultimedia.com

Design Manager: Aaron La Porta
Designer: Heather Huether

Printed in Canada

Table of Contents

Overview and Suggestions for Use V

Chapter 1   The Key to God's Storehouse 1

Chapter 2   A Glimpse of His Greatness 21

Chapter 3   God's Glory 43

Chapter 4   Order, Glory, Judgment 63

Chapter 5   Delayed Judgment 87

Chapter 6   The Coming Glory 107

Chapter 7   From Glory to Glory 125

Chapter 8   Intimate Friendship 145

HELPFUL TIPS TO MAKE
THE MOST OF YOUR STUDY

Welcome to *The Fear of the Lord Devotional Workbook*! We're delighted and grateful you have selected this valuable study. Many hours of prayer, research and preparation have been invested to make an in-depth, interactive, and life-giving experience for you.

Each of the eight chapters is directly linked to its corresponding DVD session and contains a series of candid, thought-provoking questions, inspiring devotionals, and prayers.

Each chapter also includes features like...
- **Life-Transforming Scriptures** – we encourage you to take time to meditate on the message of these verses. Nothing will leave a more lasting impression than the living Word of God.

- **Declaring His Greatness** – words of wisdom and praise from fellow believers. Scripture says that in the multitude of counselors there is safety, so take time to hear their hearts.

- **John's Quotes** – power points from the DVD sessions that are definitely worth remembering. Carefully review these statements that highlight the heart of each lesson.

- **Right Where You Live** – a special activity incorporating the session's main principles, designed to help you put them into practice and apply them practically in your life.

Throughout your study, you'll also discover some key definitions, interesting facts to ponder, and a section that summarizes the entire chapter—all to help you absorb and apply these powerful principles in your life.

Take time to write down any personal thoughts, feelings, ideas or insights the Holy Spirit reveals to you in the *My Journal* and *My Notes* sections at the end of each chapter. The scriptures and principles that come alive and explode on the inside of you are priceless. They will help you grow spiritually and are well worth investing the time to jot down for future review.

We also suggest you…
- **BEGIN AND END WITH PRAYER.** With each chapter, invite the Holy Spirit to teach you and guide you into all truth (see John 16:13). As you complete the chapter, ask Him to permanently seal in your heart what you have learned.

- **PACE YOURSELF** to complete each chapter during the week or allotted time. You may do it as part of your daily routine or work on it two or three nights a week. This is your *personal* study with the Lord, so develop the routine that works best for you.

- **BE CONSISTENT & COMMITTED.** Whatever time and place you choose to do your study, stick to it. If you fall behind, don't quit. *Press on* to the end. God will faithfully bless your every effort.

- **BE HONEST** with yourself and God as you answer each question. Knowing the truth of God's Word and the truth about yourself will bring freedom to your life that can be found no other way.

May this study on *The Fear of the Lord* liberate your spirit and unite you in a deeper, more intimate relationship with God than ever before. May your eyes be opened to a whole new dimension of His greatness, and may you be empowered by His Spirit to shine forth His glory to the generation in which we live!

> Arise! Shine! Your light has come, and the glory of the Lord has dawned. Darkness now covers the earth, and thick darkness covers the nations. But the Lord dawns, and his glory appears over you. Nations will come to your light, and kings will come to the brightness of your dawn.
> —*Isaiah 60:1-3* GW

Suggestions for Curriculum Group Leaders

To get the richest possible experience from this curriculum, we strongly encourage each group member to have their own book and workbook. This allows for more personal, in-depth study and reflection. When taking classes in school, we quickly realize the benefit of not only listening to the lectures but also reading the textbooks, taking notes and completing assignments that aid in the learning process. The same is true here; you will benefit from all of your effort, leading to more growth and revelation knowledge!

Our workbooks are designed to challenge the participants to apply the principles and ideas to their own lives. We have also made them more group-friendly by suggesting questions more suitable for group discussion. Those flagged with a [G] throughout the chapters are recommended, although it is up to your discretion as the leader.

We encourage you to prayerfully consider how to facilitate your meetings. Below are three different options in no order of importance. Our greatest suggestion is that you make this study *yours*—whatever that looks like and whatever is best for your group.

Option 1: Book before group meeting, DVD, workbook as discussion
Prior to the group meeting, have participants read the corresponding chapters in the book (see the first page of each workbook chapter). Assemble your group and watch the first DVD session. Then, take time to discuss it. (*Optional:* Use the workbook as a guide to facilitate group discussion. We encourage you to focus on the questions flagged with a [G], but feel free as the leader to choose which questions are most fitting for your group.) During the following week (the week between sessions 1 and 2), have your group complete all or the remaining portion of the workbook chapter. Follow this pattern each week.

Option 2: DVD, workbook as discussion, book & workbook as homework
Assemble your group and have them watch the first DVD session without having them read the book or complete the workbook chapter before the meeting. We recommend that you hand out the book and workbook after the group views session 1. After completing the DVD session, take time to discuss it, using the workbook as a guide to facilitate group discussion. Don't feel pressured to finish the workbook during this time. During the following week, have your group read the corresponding chapters in the book and complete any unaddressed questions in the workbook chapter. Follow this pattern each week.

Option 3: DVD, book & workbook as homework, discussion at start of next meeting
Assemble your group and watch the first DVD session. After completing the DVD session, take time to discuss it. During the following week, have your group read the corresponding chapters in the book and complete the workbook chapter. At the beginning of week 2, take time to discuss the workbook questions and any other questions or comments participants may have. Then, watch DVD session 2. Follow this pattern each week.

*He {the Lord} will be the sure foundation
for your times, a rich store {house} of salvation
and wisdom and knowledge;* **the fear
of the Lord** *is the key to this treasure.*

—Isaiah 33:6 NIV
[emphasis added]

THE KEY TO GOD'S STOREHOUSE

Please refer to session 1 of the teaching series, along with the Introduction, chapters 11, 13 and 14 in *The Fear of the Lord* book.

> "I always knew that the love of God is a foundation for our Christian walk. However, what I didn't realize until after I cried out to God is that the fear of the Lord is also a foundation for our walk with Him. What keeps Jesus as our Lord is the foundation of *the fear of the Lord*."
>
> JOHN BEVERE

[G] [1] Right now, at the start of this study, briefly describe what you understand the fear of the Lord to be.

I understand that the fear of the Lord is...

Rick - incredible adulation

Nancy - an awesome view of God that makes you want to please Him more than anything else

asking God

2 The best place to look for a definition of the fear of the Lord is in the Word itself. The Bible contains hundreds of verses from Genesis to Revelation that talk about this amazing truth. Take a few moments to meditate on these selected scriptures. Then, jot down how they help define the fear of the Lord for you.

> ...What does the Lord your God require of you but [reverently] to *fear the Lord your God*, [that is] to walk in all His ways, and to love Him, and to serve the Lord your God with all your [mind and] heart and with your entire being, to keep the commandments of the Lord and His statutes which I command you today for your good?
> —Deuteronomy 10:12-13 AMP

> And this is what he says to all humanity: "The *fear of the Lord* is true wisdom; to forsake evil is real understanding."
> —Job 28:28 NLT

> You who *fear the Lord*, praise Him; all you descendants of Jacob, glorify Him, and stand in awe of Him, all you descendants of Israel.
> —Psalm 22:23 NASB

> The *fear of the Lord* is to hate evil; pride and arrogance and the evil way and the perverse mouth I hate.
> —Proverbs 8:13 NKJV
> [emphasis added]

From these verses I can see that fearing the Lord includes...

Rick - walk in His ways, love Him, serve Him w/ mind, heart & being & keep His statutes; true wisdom; stand in awe & praise Him; hate evil, like ↓ pride, arrogance & evil mouth

Nancy - obey, love, serve w/ mind & heart; true wisdom; stand in awe, praise, glorify; hate evil

> "God has a storehouse, and the key to unlocking the treasures in His storehouse is the fear of the Lord. The treasures in His storehouse include salvation, wisdom and knowledge."
>
> JOHN BEVERE

3. From Isaiah 33:6, our opening scripture, we see that the priceless treasures of *salvation*, *wisdom*, and *knowledge* come through the fear of the Lord.

   > **Think About It**
   >
   > Have you ever been to Niagara Falls or the Grand Canyon? When you're close to the edge of the falls, enveloped by the thunder and spray of six million cubic feet of water bursting over the falls every minute, or when you stand at the rim of the canyon and a sense of dizzying awe overwhelms you as you step back from the edge of that vast expanse and bottomless gorge—that is somewhat akin to the "fear of God." It isn't an unhealthy fear, but an overwhelming sense of God Himself.[1]

   a. Read Acts 10:34-35; 13:26 and Psalm 85:8-9 and write what the Lord reveals to you concerning how the fear of the Lord opens the door to salvation.

   God gives salvation to those who fear Him regardless of background, race, ethnicity, etc.

   Related Scripture: Psalm 103:17-18.

   b. *Meditate on the message* of Proverbs 2:1-6 and explain how the fear of God is connected to receiving wisdom, knowledge, and understanding.

   More of a seeking & yearning with all your heart. Only after doing all this do you understand the fear of God.

   Related Scriptures: Proverbs 1:7; 9:10-11; 15:33.

   c. Worldly wisdom and godly wisdom that comes through the fear of the Lord are two different things. Read James 3:13-17 and describe what godly wisdom is.

   Godly wisdom is shown thru a good life & deeds done in humility. Its pure, peace-loving, considerate, submissive, full of mercy and good fruit, impartial & sincere.

> ## Declaring
> # HIS GREATNESS
>
> "To fear God is to be awe-struck with God's character and Word. It is a state of deep reverence that can cause us to tremble before Him because of His righteous judgments. The fear of the Lord is also joyful praise and worship of His glory, resulting in humble obedience to His will. 'Holy fear...is God-given, enabling men to reverence God's authority, obey His commandments, and hate and shun all form of evil.'"
>
> —Neil T. Anderson
> & Rich Miller²

Skilled living gets its start in the Fear-of-GOD, insight into life from knowing a Holy God. It's through me, Lady Wisdom, that your life deepens, and the years of your life ripen.

—Proverbs 9:10-11 The Message

4. Are you in a situation right now in which you need deliverance (salvation)? Do you need knowledge or wisdom on how to handle things?

   a. Briefly describe the situation you are facing.
      Rick

   Nancy - I'm stuck in Parkinson's, Glaucoma, + need deliverance from them to see how to get on with life.

   b. Pray and ask God for wisdom on what to do. *Prayer* is an expression of the fear of the Lord. Jot down any changes the Lord prompts you to make in your attitude or actions.
      Rick -

      Nancy -

> "Proverbs says that when you treasure God's Word and cry out for wisdom and understanding, 'Then you will understand the fear of the Lord, and find the *knowledge of God*' (2:5). What does the 'knowledge of God' mean? It means you will know God intimately and know things as God knows them. In other words, you will have the mind of Christ and see things the way God sees them."
>
> JOHN BEVERE

G 5. God is just but He is also merciful. He kindly warns us through His Word and other people whenever we are in disobedience and headed for danger (see Amos 3:7). That is what He did with Lot before He destroyed Sodom, as well as the people of Nineveh.

a. What was the difference in the way Lot's soon-to-be sons-in-law responded to God's warning and the way the people of Nineveh responded?

Lot's sons-in-law-to-be laughed & thought he was joking. The people of Nineveh repented & believed God.

Check out these important examples in Genesis 19:12-14 and Jonah 3.

b. What do these two examples from Scripture speak to your heart?

It doesn't matter who you are, when God calls, listen & respond

For as we cannot look at the sun for its brightness when the winds have cleared away the clouds, neither can we gaze at the terrible majesty of God breaking forth upon us from heaven, clothed in dazzling splendor. We cannot imagine the power of the Almighty, and yet he is so just and merciful that he does not destroy us. No wonder men everywhere fear him!

—Job 37:21-24 TLB

6. Rahab gives us a great example of a healthy fear of the Lord and seeking His mercy. Read her amazing story in Joshua 2, paying close attention to her actions in verses 9-11.

   a. How was Rahab's reaction different than the rest of the people of Jericho?

   She acknowledged that the Lord was God of heaven & earth.

   b. What else does God have to say about this woman who reverently feared the Lord?

   She was in the line of Jesus, great-great grandmother of David. She was righteous & had faith.

   Check out Hebrews 11:31; James 2:25; Matthew 1:5.

   c. What can you learn from her life and apply in your own?

   Rick — It's good to fear the Lord because He rewards you.

   Nancy — She had faith in God & acted on that faith. As she revered God, He honored her. Do I, how do I act on my faith?

Declaring HIS GREATNESS

"'Fear,' said he, 'the Lord, and keep his commandments. For if you keep the commandments of God, you will be powerful in every action. Every one of your actions will be incomparable, for fearing the Lord you will do all things well. This is the fear that you ought to have, that you may be saved. But don't fear the devil, for fearing the Lord you will have dominion over the devil, for there is no power in him.'"

—*Shepherd of Hermas* II:7

---

7. G. A person with *no* fear of God leads a very undesirable life. Read these passages and identify the behavior of a person who has no fear of God and the consequences he will ultimately receive as a result.

Therefore, having these promises, beloved, let us cleanse ourselves from all filthiness of the flesh and spirit, perfecting holiness in *the fear of God*.   *no holiness*

—*2 Corinthians 7:1* NKJV

And I say to you, My friends, do not be afraid of those who kill the body, and after that have no more that they can do. But I will show you whom you should fear: *Fear Him* who, after He has killed, has power to cast into hell; yes, I say to you, *fear Him*!

—*Luke 12:4-5* NKJV

Show proper respect *(no)* to everyone: Love the brotherhood of believers, *fear God*, honor the king.

—*1 Peter 2:17* NIV

So you must live as God's obedient children. Don't slip back into your old ways of living to satisfy your own desires. You didn't know any better then. But now you must be holy in everything you do, just as God who chose you is holy. For the Scriptures say, "You must be holy because I am holy." And remember that the heavenly Father to whom you pray has no favorites. He will judge or reward you according to what you do. So you must *live in reverent fear* of him *(no)* *(God)* during your time as "foreigners in the land."

—*1 Peter 1:14-17* NLT
[emphasis added]

a. After reading these verses, how has your mindset been challenged about the fear of the Lord being an Old Testament vs. New Testament teaching?

fear of the Lord is in both

b. As a New Testament believer, what do these verses speak to you about the importance of fearing the Lord?

We are to fear God – it's not optional

Related scriptures: Colossians 3:1-10; Hebrews 12:28-29; Revelation 14:7.

FEAR

The original Greek words used for *fear*, in connection with the fear of the Lord, throughout most of the New Testament are *phobos* and *phobeo*. They generally mean "alarm, fright, or terror" and carry the idea of "being in awe of or having reverence."[4]

The fear of the Lord is produced in the soul by the Holy Spirit. Godly fear means we dread displeasing Him, desire His favor, revere His holiness, submit to His will, are grateful for His benefits, sincerely worship Him, and conscientiously obey His commandments. Great blessings are promised upon those who have it.[5]

Note: *Fear* and *love* must coexist in us in order that both passions may be healthy and that we may please and rightly serve God.[6]

8. Explain how the fear of the Lord is different from being afraid of God.

You don't love what you're afraid of. Fear is not terror fear. You can't rightly honor good or worship what you're afraid of

Check out Genesis 3:8-10 for an example.

KNOWLEDGE

The word *knowledge* is defined in the *Dictionary of Biblical Languages* as "information of a person, with a strong implication of relationship to the person." Similarly, *Vine's Complete Expository Dictionary* says that the word *knowledge* means "to have intimate experiential knowledge of God."[7]

> "The fear of the Lord is the foundation of *intimacy with God*. This is made clear in the beginning of the book of Proverbs. It says, 'The fear of the Lord is the beginning [foundation] of knowledge' (Proverbs 1:7). What is the 'knowledge of God'? It is to know God *intimately* and know things as He knows them."
>
> — JOHN BEVERE

THE KEY TO GOD'S STOREHOUSE | 9

9 The greatest blessing of having the fear of the Lord in our hearts is the privilege of intimacy with Him. Think of it... The God of all creation extends an invitation to fellowship with Him and be His friend! There is *nothing* greater!

Meditate on the Message
Look! Here I stand at the door and knock. If you hear me calling and open the door, I will come in, and we will share a meal as friends.
—*Revelation* 3:20 NLT

...The Spirit Whom He has caused to dwell in us yearns over us and He yearns for the Spirit [to be welcome] with a jealous love.
—*James* 4:5 AMP

The secret [of the sweet, satisfying companionship] of the Lord have they who fear (revere and worship) Him, and He will show them His covenant and reveal to them its [deep, inner] meaning.
—*Psalm* 25:14 AMP

a. After reading James 4:5 and Jesus' words in Revelation 3:20, how would you explain God's heart toward you, and how does it encourage—and challenge you?
More than anything else, God desires a relat w/ ea of us - more than our purpose, needs, etc. It makes me want to respond in kind & obey.

b. In your own words, explain what the Lord is saying to you in Psalm 25:14.
Like a close friend whom you would share deep things with only, is the Lord to us & vice versa.

10 The fear of the Lord is the key to having the mind of Christ, to getting the "God's-eye view." In which situation(s) do you currently need God's perspective?
1) healing & medicine, medical community
2) relat w/ Rick

Get quiet before the Lord and present your requests to Him, believing in faith that He will give you eyes to see your situation(s) the way He does. Then, respond in obedience to any action He prompts you to take concerning it.

> ### Declaring
> # HIS GREATNESS
>
> "**Life** is in Me, and I can give it to thee only in the solitary relationship. Seek that place in Me where no other can intrude. Thou wilt find Me there, and in finding Me thus, ye shall discover all other lacks fulfilled; for in Me there is abundant Life, and with Me there are only joys, and this forever."
>
> —Frances J. Roberts[5]

11. What would you do if you saw the Lord in the splendor of His glory? Two men in Scripture, Isaiah and the apostle John, experienced this. Read their accounts, noting how each responded. Now put yourself in their shoes and briefly describe how you think you would respond. Write any insights the Lord reveals to you.

Isaiah sees the Lord – Isaiah 6:1-8
John sees the Lord – Revelation 1:10-18

totally blown away

Up until John's exile on the island of Patmos, he only knew Jesus as the miracle-working Messiah. But when Jesus appeared to him and revealed His revelation, John got a whole new glimpse of Jesus he had never seen before. For the first time, he saw Christ as the Great Creator, King of kings, and Eternal Judge of heaven and earth. Do you want to see Jesus in a new light? Do you desire a fresh revelation of the fear of the Lord? *Yes*

Pray this prayer of renewal:
> *Lord, I want to experience the blessed life that comes from fearing You. Refresh the screen of my heart with a brand-new picture of who You are. Deposit within me a clearer understanding of what it means to wholeheartedly fear You. Give me the desire and power to delight in the fear of You just as Jesus did (see Isaiah 11:1-3). I open my life up to You. Teach me. I love You, Lord, and thank You for hearing and answering my prayer...in Jesus' name, amen.*

THE FEAR OF THE LORD INCLUDES...

- A profound and abiding respect and reverence of God and all things He declares holy.
- Assigning God Most High the infinite and highest place of honor in your life.
- Deeply appreciating the privilege of His presence and the wonder of His Word.
- Worshiping God alone with passionate praise and continual thanksgiving.
- Honoring what He honors, loving what He loves, and hating what He hates. It is to make His main thing our main thing.
- Having an internal yearning to please God and not offend Him. This tempering makes it impossible for the individual to sin casually or persistently.
- Submitting of your will to embrace His fully.
- The fear of the Lord is a cleansing or purifying agent that endures forever. It is a manifestation of the Holy Spirit and Jesus' delight. There is absolutely nothing corrupt or deceitful about it.

The Blessings of Fearing God

How happy are those who fear the Lord—all who follow his ways! You will enjoy the fruit of your labor. How happy you will be! How rich your life! Your wife will be like a fruitful vine, flourishing within your home. And look at all those children! There they sit around your table as vigorous and healthy as young olive trees. That is the Lord's reward for those who fear him.

—*Psalm 128:1-4* NLT

Blessed (happy, fortunate, and to be envied) is the man who reverently and worshipfully fears [the Lord] at all times [regardless of circumstances].

—*Proverbs 28:14* AMP

Oh, how great is Your goodness, which You have laid up for those who fear You, which You have prepared for those who trust in You in the presence of the sons of men!

—*Psalm 31:19* NKJV

> **Weekly Activity 1**
>
> *Right Where You Live*
> # BECOME AN INSTRUMENT OF RESTORATION!

> *God-of-the-Angel-Armies will step in and take care of his flock, the people of Judah. He'll revive their spirits, make them proud to be on God's side. God will use them in his work of rebuilding, use them as foundations and pillars, use them as **tools** and **instruments**, use them to oversee his work. They'll be a workforce to be proud of, working as one, their heads held high.*
>
> —Zechariah 10:3-5 The Message
> [emphasis added]

Without question, we need a fresh revelation of the fear of the Lord. In America, decadence and depravity seem to abound. The fear of the Lord has greatly diminished, allowing the lines between right and wrong to be blurred and sapping us of God's supernatural strength.

As a believer, you hold a key to seeing this change. And that key is *prayer*. God is looking for *His people* to fervently, sincerely, and consistently seek His face. He is not waiting for the atheists, agnostics, or people of any other religions to seek Him—He is looking for those who call Him "Lord" to cry out on behalf of the land.

> "It is important for the church to keep the *fear of the Lord* before this nation. It is the fear of the Lord that perfects holiness in our lives. We will see a greater harvest of souls when this nation sees the church walking in the fear of the Lord."
>
> JOHN BEVERE

Take the challenge!
For the next 30 days, commit to pray for the people of America for at least 5 to 15 minutes daily. Pray that the foundations of the *fear of the Lord* and the *truth of His Word* will be rediscovered and restored, starting in your own life. Pray for the people in...

Your Family	Your Community
Your Church	Your State
Your Workplace	Your Country

Sample prayer of intercession

Father, I repent of my sins and the sins of the people of my country. Please forgive us for breaking Your commandments—calling wrong "right" and right "wrong," oppressing the poor, corrupting justice, and putting material possessions, personal success, and many other things in the place You rightly deserve. I ask You to intervene in mercy. Wash us clean by the precious blood of Jesus. Restore the foundations of the fear of the Lord and the truth of Your Word to every citizen in society. Purge Your church of impurity, complacency, selfishness, rebellion, and error. Give us new hearts that are soft and sensitive to Your touch. Thank You, God, for hearing me...in Jesus' name, amen.

This prayer is based on Scripture, including 2 Chronicles 7:13-15; Daniel 9:3-19; and Ezekiel 36:25-27.

Your prayers *will* make a difference! Ask the Lord to show you how He is moving in response to your intercession. Jot down what He reveals in the *My Notes* section at the end of this chapter. This will increase your faith and the faith of others as you share it. "The Lord blesses each nation that worships only him. He blesses his chosen ones" (Psalm 33:12 CEV).

[G] NOTE TO GROUP LEADERS: To begin "The Challenge," you may find it beneficial to pray through the list as a group. What a better way to start the 30 days than with powerful group prayer! If time allows, you may also want to pray collectively at each of the following group meetings during the 30 days.

| Weekly Devotional 1 | ## THE RIGHT FOUNDATION |

*Fear of the Lord is the **foundation** of true wisdom. All who obey his commandments will grow in wisdom. Praise him forever!*

—Psalm 111:10 NLT
[emphasis added]

Every house and every building need a strong, solid foundation. Although it is virtually unseen, once the construction is complete, its role is critical to the quality and strength of the structure. If the foundation is unstable, made of compromised materials or filled with flaws, it is only a matter of time until the construction crumbles.

Similarly, you need a strong, solid foundation as a follower of Christ. As concrete and rebar wire work together to make a well-built physical foundation, the *love of God* and the *fear of the Lord* work together to make a well-built spiritual foundation. To build your Christian life on the foundation of the love of God *alone* would be like eliminating the network of wire that runs through and reinforces the concrete. Things may be fine for a while, but when the full weight of living begins to stress the "slab" of your soul and spirit, your foundation will falter.

> "The foundation is so important. You can build a house and have the best marble, the most beautiful windows, and the best of everything in it. But, if it is not built on a solid foundation, when a strong enough storm comes, that house will fall and great will be its fall. It doesn't matter how nice your Christian life is or how effective it is; if you don't have the right foundation, the bigger the house, the greater the fall. The right foundation is *the fear of the Lord*."
>
> **JOHN BEVERE**

Stop and think. Initially, how did knowing that *God loves you* and that He gave His only Son, Jesus, to die in your place impact your choice to surrender your life to Him?

R - *A lot*

N - *I don't think I really understood it at first*

How does the knowledge and revelation of His love help you *stay connected* in a pure relationship with Him?

R - *Its imp + the basic reason for being connected*

N - *Where else can I go to get a better relat?*

THE KEY TO GOD'S STOREHOUSE | 15

> *Your love, God, is my song, and I'll sing it! I'm forever telling everyone how faithful you are. I'll never quit telling the story of your love—how you built the cosmos and guaranteed everything in it. Your love has always been our lives' foundation, your fidelity has been the roof over our world.*
>
> —Psalm 89:1-2 MSG
> [emphasis added]

Did the fear of the Lord influence you initially to repent of your sins and surrender your life to Him? If so, how?

R- I didn't understand what fear was
N-

How does having a healthy fear of the Lord compel you to *stay pure* in your walk with Him?

R- I want to please him in my inner being, suppress impure thoughts

> *Through skillful and godly Wisdom is a house (a life, a home, a family) built, and by understanding it is established [on a sound and good foundation].*
>
> —Proverbs 24:3 AMP
> [emphasis added]

What does Jesus have to say about the foundation of your life? Read through and meditate on His words in this passage, and then answer the questions that follow.

These words I speak to you are not mere additions to your life, homeowner improvements to your standard of living. They are **foundation** words,

words to build a life on. If you work the words into your life, you are like a smart carpenter who dug deep and laid the foundation of his house on bedrock. When the river burst its banks and crashed against the house, nothing could shake it; it was built to last. But if you just use my words in Bible studies and don't work them into your life, you are like a dumb carpenter who built a house but skipped the foundation. When the swollen river came crashing in, it collapsed like a house of cards. It was a total loss.
—*Luke* 6:47-49 MSG
[emphasis added]

What is the Holy Spirit speaking to you through this passage? What is He showing you about your spiritual foundation?

R- I need to be more committed to Him.

N- My life needs to be built on the fear of God - putting into practice what I read.

At this time, is there anything in your life hindering you from finding firm footing on the Solid Rock, Jesus Christ? If so, what is it? Surrender these things to the Lord in prayer, knowing that He loves you greatly and wants to be close to you.

R- No

N- I see Rick & us and get distracted instead of looking to Jesus

"Remember, there is only one **foundation**, the one already laid: Jesus Christ. Take particular care in picking out your building materials. Eventually there is going to be an inspection. If you use cheap or inferior materials, you'll be found out. The inspection will be thorough and rigorous. You won't get by with a thing" (1 Corinthians 3:11-13 The Message, emphasis added). So, build your life on the solid and sure foundation of God's unchanging Word and the fear of the Lord. There is no substitute!

My Journal
THINGS I WANT TO REMEMBER

> "Remember, the fear of the Lord is **not** to be frightened or afraid of God. If you are frightened of God, you will withdraw from Him. How can you have a relationship of intimacy with God if you are scared of Him? And that is what God passionately desires—an intimate, passionate relationship with you and every one of us."
>
> JOHN BEVERE

As you come to the close of this first chapter, take a few moments to quietly reflect upon the new insights God's Spirit is revealing to you. What is He showing you that you have never seen before? In what ways is He challenging you to change? Don't rush through this pivotal point in your journey. Take time to write what you are sensing Him speak to your heart.

3-23-11

R - Challenging me to change

N - Keep my eyes on Jesus - not Rick, distractions. Put His words into practice. Develop the discipline of daily time w/ God.

Chapter 1 - Fear of the Lord - the base, foundation
 - key to intimate relat w/ God

CHAPTER OVERVIEW

Along with the love of God, the *fear of the Lord* is the most important foundational element of our Christian walk. It is a wonderful work produced by the Holy Spirit, empowering us to avoid evil, obey God's commands, and live intimately with Him every day. It is not only the beginning of wisdom and knowledge, but also the key to God's storehouse of blessings. Although its definition is far-reaching, it is basically a deep overriding awe and reverence for God, His Word, and His unsearchable ways. It is through the fear of the Lord that we are able to grow and mature in holiness.

(1) *Nelson's Annual Preacher's Sourcebook 2002 Edition*, Robert J. Morgan, Editor (Nashville TN: Thomas Nelson Publishers, 2001) p. 114. (2) Neil T. Anderson & Rich Miller, *Freedom from Fear* (Eugene, OR: Harvest House Publishers, 1999) p. 237). (3) Quotes on *Fear of God* (http://www.christian-history.org/fear-of-god-quotes.html, retrieved 9-23-10). (4) Adapted from *Strong's Exhaustive Concordance of the Bible*, James Strong, LL.D., S.T.D. (Nashville, TN: Thomas Nelson Publishers, 1990). (5) Adapted from *The New Unger's Bible Dictionary*, Merrill F. Unger (Chicago, IL: Moody Press, Revised and Updated Edition, 1988). (6) Ibid. (7) John Bevere, *Drawing Near* (Nashville, TN: Thomas Nelson, Inc., 2004) pp. 87-88. (8) Frances J. Roberts, *Come Away My Beloved* (Ojai, CA: King's Farspan, Inc., 1973) p. 181.

My Notes

3-17-11

Key to God's Storehouse
  foundation - fear of L   Is. 33:6
              - most imp
   wisdom   P 111:10
   know   Prov 1:7
               2:5

fear - photos
Ps 19:9 - fear of L is clean, enduring forever

fear of Lord = not frightened
               profound respect

3-24-11

- Kerry + Jo - salvation - surround w/ believers
- Nan's diabetes, knees
Prayer - travel safety for Cully's kids - Kyle & Rona
- finish healing for Ken
- healing for Rick's eyes, Parkinson's
- cont healing for Rosalie
- Cully's back, hearing
- Mel's hearing
- Debbie's asthma, allergies

*Search high and low, scan skies and land;
you'll find nothing and no one quite like GOD.
God is greatly to be feared in the assembly of the saints,
and to be held in reverence by all those around Him.*

—Psalm 89:6-7
Verse 6, The Message; Verse 7, NKJV
[emphasis added]

3·24

Cully - Kim & Diane Turner, Parkinsons, heart
Rick - healing of eye, Parkinsons, vision
Ken - healing
Rosalie - healing, strength, endurance + balance
Mel - hearing
Church - prepare for acceptance of God's glory
   - need pastor (Cully's) transition - Word of Life
   - pastor + leaders prepare

[Handwritten notes at top: fear of God limited to understanding of His greatness. 2 ways to search out God's greatness 1) in spirits, 2 Corin 4:6 2) in creation - Ps 145:10-11]

2

A GLIMPSE OF HIS GREATNESS

Please refer to session 2 of the teaching series, along with chapters 1, 3 and 12 in *The Fear of the Lord* book.

> "Your fear of God is limited to your *understanding of His greatness*. Moses knew how important it is to understand the greatness of God because that is what keeps us in the place of reverentially fearing Him. The more extensive our comprehension of God's greatness—although in itself is incomprehensible—the greater our capacity to fear Him."
>
> JOHN BEVERE

[G] 1 God's greatness is unsearchable! And yet, He gives us glimpses of it in His creation as well as through a direct revelation of Himself in our spirit. That's what 2 Corinthians 4:6 NIV means when it says that God "…made his light shine in our hearts to give us *the light of the knowledge of the glory of God* in the face of Christ" (emphasis added).

a. Can you recall a time when God made His glory and greatness very real in your spirit? If so, describe it. How did it make you feel, and how did you respond?

[Handwritten: Rick - when saw "Truth Project" Nancy - stars at night at Lake Peregin]

b. How is this experience still impacting you today?

Rick - confirms my faith
Nancy -

*O Sovereign Lord, you have only begun to show your **greatness** and the strength of your hand to me, your servant. Is there any god in heaven or on earth who can perform such great and mighty deeds as you do?*

—Deuteronomy 3:24 NLT
[emphasis added]

GREATNESS

In the Old Testament, there are a few Hebrew words and derivatives of those words that are used to describe God's *greatness*. Four primary ones are *godel*, *geduwllah*, *rob*, and *rebuw*. Together, they carry the meaning of "magnitude, magnify, exceed, mighty acts, majesty, abundantly excellent."[1] In the New Testament, the word *greatness* is primarily taken from two Greek words *megethos*, meaning "the power of God," and *huperbole*, meaning "the surpassing excellencies of God."[2]

---

2. The greatness, or glory, of God is inseparably linked to His presence. By seeking His presence, we can better understand His greatness. In Scripture, there are two types, or expressions, of God's presence noted—His *omnipresence* and His *manifest presence*.

   a. Read these verses and briefly describe the **omnipresence** of God.

   Psalm 139:7-10 • Proverbs 15:3 • Jeremiah 23:23-24 • Matthew 28:20

   1 - God is everywhere 2 - God sees everything 3 - God fills heaven + earth 4 - God fills time

A GLIMPSE OF HIS GREATNESS | 23

b. Check out these examples in Scripture. From these, how would you describe the **manifest presence** (glory) of God? How is it different from His omnipresence?

Psalm 85:9 • 2 Chronicles 7:1-6 • John 11:38-45 • Acts 2:1-12

1- His glory dwells in the land of those who fear Him 2- His glory filled the temple 3- God's glory was a resurrected life 4- God's glory was seen in tongues of fire + heard in a violent wind + speaking in different tongues

---

MANIFEST

The Greek words for *manifest* in the New Testament mean "to make visible or clear, to bring out in open sight, or to shine."³ Webster defines *manifest* as "to reveal, to show plainly, to make public, or to disclose to the eye or to the understanding."⁴ When God's presence *manifests*, His greatness is revealed openly for all to see. Not only can people in attendance see it with their eyes, but many can also better understand His greatness in their hearts.

---

*Surely His salvation is near to those who reverently and worshipfully fear Him, [and is ready to be appropriated] that [the **manifest presence** of God, His] glory may tabernacle and abide in our land.*

—Psalm 85:9 AMP
[emphasis added]

[G] 3 John shared how the people at a gathering in Brazil behaved during the beginning of a church service. Their lack of reverential fear for God caused them to miss out on the manifest presence of God. Ironically, they were not even aware of it.

DO YOU HAVE REVERENCE FOR GOD IN HIS HOUSE?
How Is Your…

ARRIVAL TIME: How important is it for you to get to church on time? Do you sometimes miss worship altogether? Or, do you make it a point to get in and get seated before the service begins?

We try to be on time, but usually we get there when we get there

PARTICIPATION: When it comes to singing praise and worship, are you a spectator or a participant? Are you disconnected from what is going on? Or, are you actively engaged in worship?

Rick - spotted
Nan - I participate; degree varies

ATTENTIVENESS: Where is your focus when your pastor is ministering? Are you reading the bulletin, thinking about where and what to eat for lunch, or contemplating the "big game" that starts at noon? Or, are you attentively following along?

Rick - sometimes I'm engaged, sometimes distracted. I'm mostly trying to be engaged
Nan - I take notes to be more attentive; this is what I come for

DEPARTURE TIME: How eager are you to leave? Do you get up and go during the closing prayer time? Or, do you stay put, hungry for God to move in your life and the lives of others?

Rick - I'm anxious to go

Nancy - I look for peop to connect w/ - if no one I leave

In light of your answers, how would describe your *fear of the Lord* when it comes to His house? In what ways do you feel like He is asking you to rise to the next level?

Rick - I'm not fearful - connect w/ people more - be more engaged in sermon - make more effort to get there early

Nan - I want to make all of it more of a priority - be there on time; worship Him, get God's message for me out of the sermon + look to whom He would have me connect w/ afterwards

> "Psalm 89:7 says, 'God is greatly to be feared in the assembly of the saints, and to be held in reverence by all those around Him' (NKJV). You will never find God's *manifest presence* in an atmosphere where He is not held in the utmost of respect."
>
> JOHN BEVERE

*The person who has My commands and keeps them is the one who [really] loves Me; and whoever [really] loves Me will be loved by My Father, and I [too] will love him and will show (reveal, **manifest**) Myself to him. [I will let Myself be clearly seen by him and make Myself real to him.]*

—John 14:21 AMP
[emphasis added]

4 After hearing teaching on the fear of the Lord, the people in the Brazilian arena repented for their attitudes and experienced a wonderful visitation of the Lord's presence—a manifestation so powerful people talked about it for years.

a. When we demonstrate our love for Jesus by keeping His commands, He manifests Himself to us. What amazing gift has God given us to help us obey and please Him?

~~the Holy Spirit~~ God's grace

Check out 1 Corinthians 15:10; James 4:6.

b. Can you remember a time when you experienced a special visitation of God's presence or when He spoke something to your heart? If so, briefly describe what happened.

Rick - When I was in surgery for DBS, both times I felt Jesus' presence with me.

Nan -

c. How did the encounter impact you? How is it still influencing your life today?

Rick – I think of it often – it's comforting – I have less fear of death

> ...*In Your presence is fullness of joy; at Your right hand are pleasures forevermore.*
>
> —Psalm 16:11 NKJV
> [emphasis added]

Declaring
HIS GREATNESS

"A believer longs after God—to come into His *presence*...to feel His love...to feel near to Him in secret...to feel in the crowd that He is nearer than all the creatures. Ah! Dear brethren, have you ever tasted this blessedness? There is greater rest and solace to be found in the presence of God for one hour, than in an eternity of the presence of man."
—*Robert Murray M'Cheyne*

---

5 G Imagine this: You are sitting in a room and suddenly your all-time favorite sports hero, musician, actor/actress, or minister walks in. Much to your amazement, they come and stand just a few feet in front of you, look you straight in the eye, and begin talking.

a. How would you respond to being in their presence? How would you respond to them directly? How valuable would their words be?

Rick – Ron Reagan – honored + tongue-tied; I'd value them

Nan – A Lincoln or Robt E Lee – " " ; " "them

b. When you spend time with your spouse or a good friend, what do you like them to do to show that they value your company and are interested in what you have to say?

Rick – Mel – listens to me

Nancy – Kim – not be rushed, ask how I am + listens + responds to what I say

c. Looking at your previous answers, how can you rise to the next level in valuing your alone time with the Lord?

Rick - I need to listen to what the H.S. has to say

Nan - I need to listen + value what God has to say

> *Come, let's shout praises to God, raise the roof for the Rock who saved us! Let's march into his presence singing praises, lifting the rafters with our hymns! And why? Because God is the best, High King over all the gods. In one hand he holds deep caves and caverns, in the other hand grasps the high mountains. He made Ocean—he owns it! His hands sculpted Earth! So come, let us worship: bow before him, on your knees before God, who made us! Oh yes, he's our God, and we're the people he pastures, the flock he feeds.*
>
> — Psalm 95:1-7 The Message

6. Great things happen when we reverently fear the Lord and spend intimate time in His life-transforming presence!

Meditate on the Message

For the Lord God is our *sun* and our shield. He gives us grace and glory. The Lord will withhold no good thing from those who do what is right.

—*Psalm 84:11* NLT

Then Jesus spoke to them again, saying, "I am the *light of the world.* He who follows Me shall not walk in darkness, but have the *light of life.*

—*John 8:12* NKJV

God, the blessed and only Ruler, the King of kings and Lord of lords, who alone is immortal and *who lives in unapproachable light,* whom no one has seen or can see. To him be honor and might forever. Amen.

—*1 Timothy 6:15-16* NIV
[emphasis added]

Related scriptures: Psalm 104:1-2; 2 Corinthians 4:4; James 1:17; 1 John 1:5; Revelation 1:16.

a. What recurring characteristic of God's greatness is revealed in these verses?
   His light

b. What happens when you sit in the radiating presence of God? Think about what happened to Moses after spending time in God's presence (see Exodus 34:29-35). *You would reflect God in you.*

> The Son *radiates* God's own glory and expresses the very character of God, and he sustains everything by the mighty power of his command.
> —Hebrews 1:3 NLT

> Those who look to him are *radiant*; their faces are never covered with shame.
> —Psalm 34:5 NIV

> ARISE… Shine (be *radiant* with the *glory of the Lord*), for your light has come, and the glory of the Lord has risen upon you!
> —Isaiah 60:1 AMP
> [emphasis added]

Related scriptures: Psalm 18:28-29 (1); Ecclesiastes 8:1 (2); Daniel 12:3 (3); 2 Corinthians 3:18 (4).

1 - *He turns darkness to light*
2 - *wisdom brightens a man's face*
3 - *wisdom + leading many to right. Will shine*
4 - *we're reflecting His glory + being transformed into His likeness*

Declaring HIS GREATNESS

"The most intimate union with God is the actual presence of God. Although this relationship with God is totally spiritual, it is quite dynamic, because the soul is not asleep; rather, it is powerfully excited. In this state, the soul is livelier than fire and brighter than the unclouded sun; yet, at the same time, it is tender and devout."

—Brother Lawrence[6]

7 One way to help in entering God's presence, especially when discouraged, is to reminisce and meditate on the amazing things He has done in the past (see Psalm 77:11-12; 105:5). Take a few minutes to reflect on His goodness and faithfulness—times when He rescued you from trouble, blessed you unexpectedly, and protected you from harm. Write what comes to mind.

A few memories of God's greatness to me include...

_____
_____
_____
_____

Let these memories paint a fresh picture of God's powerful, unchanging love for you!

> *Thank God! Call out his Name! Tell the whole world who he is and what he's done! Sing to him! Play songs for him! Broadcast all his wonders! Revel in his holy Name, God-seekers, be jubilant! Study God and his strength,* **seek his presence** *day and night; remember all the wonders he performed, the miracles and judgments that came out of his mouth.*
>
> —1 Chronicles 16:8-12 The Message
> [emphasis added]

[G] **8** Scripture reveals that Jesus regularly pulled away to pray and spend time in the Father's presence. He went to the mountains, deserts, sea sides, and gardens. Could it be that the beautiful surroundings revived Him and reminded Him of the Father's greatness?

a. What places in nature make you stand in an awe of God's greatness? Is it the seaside or the mountains? Is it watching the sun set or hearing the wind rustle through the trees? Is it seeing a starlit sky? Why are these things special to you?

Nan— I love vista views of the water, so beautiful, calming, restful — takes me away from troubles of the world

> ### Declaring
> # HIS GREATNESS
>
> "I love to think of nature as an unlimited broadcasting station, through which God speaks to us every hour, if we will only tune in. ...Reading about nature is fine, but if a person walks in the woods and listens carefully, he can learn more than what is in books, for they speak with the voice of God."
>
> —*George Washington Carver*[7]

b. How often do you purposely pull away to spend time with God and be refreshed? What adjustments can you make in your life that will enable you to pull away more often?

Not often – when I go for a walk now is the closest I get

> ### Think About It
>
> **Recreation.** It means "refreshment of the strength and spirits after toil." <u>Literally, recreation is to *re-create*, *reanimate*, and *revive*.</u>[8] For you, recreation may not come through visiting places in nature. Instead, going to the nursery of your local hospital and seeing the newborns may be what stirs your heart. Or, maybe it's hearing the harmony of a magnificent symphony or sitting at the airport to watch planes take off. <u>Whatever keeps the "awe" in the *awe*someness of who God is, *feed it*.</u> Take time to pull away and allow God to **re-create** the wonder of who He is in your soul and spirit again and again. Your entire life will be better because of it!

9 G There are few things the enemy will fight you on more than spending time in God's presence. He knows the power of it because he was once there. List the top three things that keep you from spending time with God, and ask Him to show you how to conquer them.

The **TOP THREE THINGS** that hinder me from spending quality time with God are…

1. _____

Nen – too much on my plate

2. _____

Nen – not planning ahead

3. *Nan - not feeling I deserve it or that it's ok for me*

To overcome these obstacles, I believe the Lord is showing me...

> ### Declaring
> ### HIS GREATNESS
>
> "God has no favorites and declares that angels will minister to all the heirs of faith. If we, the sons of God, would only realize how close His ministering angels are, what calm assurance we could have in facing the cataclysms of life."
> —*Billy Graham*[9]

Nan - 1. Better sched my time
2. Plan the day the night before
3. Realize I do deserve it

The Blessings of Fearing God

The Angel of the Lord encamps around those who fear Him [who revere and worship Him with awe] and each of them He delivers. O taste and see that the Lord [our God] is good! Blessed (happy, fortunate, to be envied) is the man who trusts and takes refuge in Him.
—*Psalm 34:7-8* AMP

All you who fear the Lord, trust the Lord! He is your helper and your shield.
—*Psalm 115:11* NLT

He fulfills the desires of those who fear him; he hears their cry and saves them.
—*Psalm 145:19* NIV

> **Weekly Activity 2**

Right Where You Live
YOU ARE FEARFULLY AND WONDERFULLY MADE!

For you created my inmost being; you knit me together in my mother's womb. I praise you because I am **fearfully and wonderfully made**; *your works are wonderful, I know that full well.*

—Psalm 139:13-14 NIV
[emphasis added]

Did you know that your life began from **one** tiny cell that was fertilized? In the nucleus of that miniscule dot, the master computer called DNA contained the genetic programming for every unique aspect of your yet-unformed adult person. Imagine…every organ, every hair, every blood vessel, every personality trait, every behavioral pattern was all programmed within the chromosomes of the DNA of that cell.[10]

Scientists today have discovered that a single cell is much more complex than originally thought. The average adult can have as many as 100 trillion cells, and each of them function as a large walled city. Think of it… Within each cell there are systems for generating energy, making food, transporting nutrients, transmitting information, protecting against enemy invasion, and disposing of waste. Amazingly, all these functions work in harmony with each other and the surrounding cells. What's even more amazing is that each cell and its systems have the ability to *replicate* themselves automatically![11] Indeed, the human body screams of God's greatness!

Clearly, **you are no accident** of random chance as some have suggested. As Dr. Michael Denton, a conservative microbiologist and a Christian, stated, "The complexity of the simplest known type of cell is so great that it is impossible to accept that such an object could have been thrown together suddenly by some kind of freakish, vastly improbable event. Such an occurrence would be indistinguishable from a miracle."[12] Denton is not the only scientist to note the miracle of life. Christian and non-Christian scientists alike have commented similarly.

Galen, perhaps the most famous and important physician during the Roman Empire, said,

"Every man who looks at things with an open mind, seeing a spirit living in this mass of flesh and humors, and examining the structure of any animal whatever...*will comprehend the excellence of the Spirit which is in heaven.*"[13]

Dr. Francis Crick, biologist and Nobel Prize winner famous for his co-discovery of DNA, stated,

"An honest man, armed with all the knowledge available to us now, could only state that in some sense, the origin of life appears at the moment to be almost a *miracle*, so many are the conditions which would have had to have been satisfied to get it going." [14]

And ironically, even **Charles Darwin**, the man most credited for the theory of evolution, said,

"To suppose that the eye, with all its inimitable contrivances for adjusting the focus to different distances, for admitting different amounts of light, and for the correction of spherical and chromatic aberration, could have been formed by natural selection, seems, I freely confess, *absurd in the highest possible degree*...."[15]

For decades, the enemy has propagated evolutionary ideas to diminish the greatness of our Creator God. But the truth of who God is has always prevailed. He is absolutely amazing, and He desires to be intimately connected in relationship with YOU!

Search out His greatness in these scriptures:
Then God said, "Let us make human beings in our image, to be like us. They will reign over the fish in the sea, the birds in the sky, the livestock, all the wild animals on the earth, and the small animals that scurry along the ground." So *God created human beings in his own image.* In the image of God he created them; male and female *he created them.*
—*Genesis 1:26-27* NLT

The Spirit of God has made me, and the breath of the Almighty gives me life.
—*Job 33:4* NKJV

Know that the Lord, He is God; *it is He who has made us,* and not we ourselves; we are His people and the sheep of His pasture.
—*Psalm 100:3* NKJV

> This is what the Lord says—*your Redeemer, who formed you in the womb*: I am the Lord, who has made all things, who alone stretched out the heavens, who spread out the earth by myself.
>
> —*Isaiah 44:24* NIV

> I knew you before *I formed you in your mother's womb*. Before you were born I set you apart and appointed you as my prophet to the nations.
>
> —*Jeremiah 1:5* NLT

> *He himself gives all men life and breath* and everything else. From one man he made every nation of men, that they should inhabit the whole earth; and he determined the times set for them and the exact places where they should live. God did this so that men would seek him and perhaps reach out for him and find him, though he is not far from each one of us.
>
> —*Acts 17:25-27* NIV
> [emphasis added]

Now, stop and think…

If you're created in the image of God, what can you have that no other part of creation can have?

the likeness of God; fellowship w/ God

Check out 1 John 1:3; John 14:23; Revelation 3:20.

How do these scriptures ignite your faith in God as your Great Creator?

He created us/me to be in relationship w/ Him.

How do they inspire a fresh reverential fear of the Lord in your heart?

I need to make time for God

Have fun doing research yourself!
Allow the "fear and wonder" of the way God created you to come alive and grow! Get a Bible concordance and search for scriptures that confirm God as Creator. You can look up key words such as: Creator, creation, created, foundations, maker, heaven and earth, heavens, stars, etc.

As you meditate on the awesomeness of God as Great Creator, you will get a new glimpse of His greatness and develop a deeper reverential fear for who He is!

Weekly Devotional 2 | INDESCRIBABLE, UNCONTAINABLE, IMMEASURABLE GOD

> *Creation and creatures applaud you, God; your holy people bless you. They talk about the glories of your rule, they exclaim over your splendor. Praise the Lord! Praise the Lord from the heavens! Praise him from the skies! Praise him, all his angels! Praise him, all the armies of heaven! Praise him, sun and moon! Praise him, all you twinkling stars! Praise him, skies above! Praise him, vapors high above the clouds! Let everything that breathes sing praises to the Lord!*
>
> —Psalm 145:10-11; 148:1-4; 150:6
> Psalm 145 The Message; Psalm 148 and 150 NLT

Our God—the one true God, Creator of heaven and earth and all that is in them—is truly amazing! He is from everlasting to everlasting—He has no beginning and no end. He is all-powerful, all-knowing, and ever-present. He never changes, yet His loving-kindness and mercy are new to us every day. Indeed, He is indescribable, uncontainable, and immeasurable!

So, how great is God to *you*? In your heart and mind, how do you see Him? If He is *not* indescribable, uncontainable, and immeasurable, you may have "boxed" Him in. The truth is that all of us limit who God is at times. That may be where you are right now. But, God doesn't want you to stay there; He wants you to *expand your expectations*! He wants you to see Him in new ways like never before. How can you do this? Start by meditating on His Word.

Ponder His greatness!
> You alone are the Lord. You made the heavens, even the highest heavens, and all their starry host, the earth and all that is on it, the seas and all

that is in them. You give life to everything, and the multitudes of heaven worship you.

—Nehemiah 9:6 NIV

You placed the world on its foundation so it would never be moved. Mountains rose and valleys sank to the levels you decreed. Then you set a firm boundary for the seas, so they would never again cover the earth.

—Psalm 104:5, 8-9 NLT

Listen to me, my people, my chosen ones! I alone am God. I am the First; I am the Last. It was my hand that laid the foundations of the earth; the palm of my right hand spread out the heavens above; I spoke and they came into being.

—Isaiah 48:12-13 TLB

Related scriptures: Psalm 33:6-9; 102:25; Isaiah 45:11-12; Acts 17:24-26.

Again and again, from Genesis to Revelation, Scripture emphatically declares that God created *everything*. Dozens of God-fearing people, who penned His Holy Word and lived on three different continents over sixteen centuries, all claimed and named God as Creator.

How do these verses invigorate your faith and instill a reverential fear of God in your heart? What do they say to *you* about His awesome character?

1- God created the earth + heavens by speaking them into existence
2- "   "   "   "   "   "
3- "   "   + He can do what He wants w/ it
4- "   "   + doesn't need man to serve Him; He gives life + breath + everything else to man; He created all men from one + set the time + location for each, so man would reach out for God.

God created all of nature, including me. He put me in this spot at this time to have fellow. w/ me + me w/ Him. He gave me all I have or ever will have, including my circumstances so I would reach out to Him. How can I do anything less!?!

Not only did God create everything, He also *maintains* everything. Colossians 1:16-17 says, "Christ himself is the Creator who made everything in heaven and earth, the things we can see and the things we can't; the spirit world with its kings and kingdoms, its rulers and authorities; all were made by Christ for his own use and glory. He was before all else began and *it is his power that holds everything together*" (TLB, emphasis added). Wow! Jesus is the invincible, invisible force keeping everything fastened in place. Not one detail is left unattended. Check out these verses declaring His greatness:

How great is our God?!

He counts the stars and calls them all by name. How great is our Lord! His power is absolute! His understanding is beyond comprehension!

—*Psalm* 147:4-5 NLT

Who has scooped up the ocean in his two hands, or measured the sky between his thumb and little finger, who has put all the earth's dirt in one of his baskets, weighed each mountain and hill?

—*Isaiah* 40:12 The Message

This is what the Lord says: "Heaven is my throne, and the earth is my footstool. …My hands have made both heaven and earth; they and everything in them are mine. I, the Lord, have spoken!"

—*Isaiah* 66:1-2 NLT

For a mind-boggling, "ear-opening" conversation, **check out** what God told Job (see Job 38 and 39).

What is God's Spirit showing you through these scriptures about the immensity of your Maker?

It's mind-boggling! I can't fathom that big! He truly deserves

Now, you may be thinking, *Yeah, God is great and powerful; but, is He really mindful of me?* That is what David asked the Lord in Psalm 8. He said, "When I look at the night sky and see the work of your fingers—the moon and the stars you set in place—what are mere mortals that you should think about them, human beings that you should care for them? Yet you made them only a little lower than God and crowned them with glory and honor" (verses 3-5 NLT).

Is the Lord mindful of you? Does He care about what you're going through? Yes! Read Luke 12:6-7, Isaiah 49:14-16, and Psalm 56:8 and write what the Lord speaks to your heart.

___

___

___

___

___

___

___

___

___

___

Friend, you are dearly loved by God. Give Him your love. Give Him your praise. He deserves it!

Prayer of praise

Who is like You, Oh Lord—Great Creator of heaven and earth? You are indescribable, uncontainable, and immeasurable! Please forgive me for boxing You in by any means. Help me to see with growing intensity the greatness of who You are. You are matchless in power, wisdom, mercy, and love. Thank you for caring for me and wanting to be in relationship with me. I am so grateful for Your guiding and protective presence in my life. Let my reverential fear of You continue to grow. I love You, Lord. You are great and greatly to be praised…in Jesus' name, amen.

My Journal
THINGS I WANT TO REMEMBER

Have you received a new glimpse of God's greatness? Has the awe and wonder of Him as Creator come alive? Take some time—don't rush—to quietly reflect upon the new insights He is revealing and all He is communicating to your heart.

God's glory - greatness 3-30-11
 Can't honor God w/out acknow His glory
Is 29:13
 root of all disobed. is lack of fear of God
 "Reduced God to calf"
Rom 1:23 glory man familiar w/
 We've served G in image we have made
Heb 4:13

1. Keep awareness that God sees/hears all
Kerri + Joe:
 -Katelyn 13 + Jesse
Kristin + Rick:
 Julia, Josie, Jessica
Dallas
Nancy's family
 Mike + Brenda
  Brandon + Holly
   Corey + Merari:
    Merari + Eli
  Brock
Rosalie's family
Errol + Karen
 Sheri + family
 Christine + family

* Make family tree
* main dish
Griffin Lobe.com

CHAPTER OVERVIEW

God wants your understanding of His greatness to grow so that your fear of Him can grow and empower you for extraordinary living. How can you better understand God's greatness? By beholding the wonders of His creation as well as receiving a direct revelation of Him in your spirit. The deeper your comprehension of God's greatness, the greater your ability to fear Him. The more you fear Him, the more you will experience His manifest presence and blessings. So, take time to pull away and seek the Lord. Learn to regularly rest in His presence. Your love for Him will grow; your fear for Him will grow. Your life will be enlarged!

---

(1) Adapted from *Strong's Exhaustive Concordance of the Bible*, James Strong, L.L.D., S.T.D. (Nashville, TN: Thomas Nelson Publishers, 1990). (2) Adapted from *Vine's Complete Expository Dictionary of Old and New Testament Words*, W. E. Vine (Nashville, TN: Thomas Nelson, Inc., 1996) p. 281, NT. (3) Ibid, p. 390 NT. (4) Adapted from *Noah Webster's First Edition of an American Dictionary of the English Language* (1828), Republished in facsimile edition by Foundation for American Christian Education (San Francisco, CA, 2000). (5) Quotes on Intimacy with God (http://dailychristianquote.com/dcqintimacy3.html, retrieved 8-27-10). (6) Brother Lawrence, *The Practice of the Presence of God* (New Kensington, PA: Whitaker House, 1982) p. 65. (7) *Standing Firm: 365 Devotionals to Strengthen Your Faith*, compiled by Patti M. Hummel (St. San Luis Obispo, CA: Parable) p. 109. (8) See note 4. (9) Billy Graham, *Angels* (Dallas, TX: Word Publishing, 1994) pp. 104-105. (10) Dennis R. Petersen, *Unlocking the Mysteries of Creation* (El Dorado, CA: Creation Resource Publications, 2002) adapted from p. 88. (11) Ibid., adapted from p. 92. (12) Ibid., p. 89. (13) John Hudson Tiner, *The History of Medicine* (Green Forest, AR: Master Books, 1999, 2009) p. 10. (14) See note 10, p. 108. (15) Ibid., p. 94.

My Notes

...*Fear God and give him glory*....
Worship him who made the heavens,
the earth, the sea and the springs of water.

—*Revelation 14:7* NIV
[emphasis added]

GOD'S GLORY

Please refer to session 3 of the teaching series, along with chapter 2 in *The Fear of the Lord* book.

> "Many today don't know and recognize the *real* Jesus revealed by the Holy Spirit. The generations who've gone before us prove that the Lord of Glory goes unrecognized when there is a lack of holy fear. The fact is, only those who fear God recognize Him! Only those who fear Him get a glimpse of His glory or greatness."
>
> JOHN BEVERE

G 1 As you can see from our first two chapters, having a healthy fear of the Lord connects us intimately in relationship with God and brings us great blessings. How does your fear of the Lord grow and remain healthy? By having an accurate image of who He is.

a. Take a few moments and describe your image of God. How do you see Him?

Rick - overpowering presence

Nan - huge, powerful, loving/giant daddy on whose lap I can sit & be enfolded in his strong, protective arms

b. In session 3 of the teaching, John gives an example of a famous leader visiting a country as a common man and going unnoticed, not getting the respect and honor he deserves. How does this relate to your relationship with the Lord? What do you think He would say of your life in regards to this?

Rick - I honor Him when I need Him. Otherwise I put Him in the bkgrd. // He would scold me

Nan - I can get so caught up in details of life I rush away on my own. Then acknow when I need Him. // Take me w/ you in everything

c. Moses, Gideon, Saul (Paul) and countless others all had life-changing encounters with God. Have you had a memorable encounter with God? If so, describe your experience(s) and tell how it shapes your life today.

Rick - brain surgeries // Feel more intense about His love for me; has increased my faith

Nan - various smaller encounters (Jerry, women's nglow, w/ Jan accepting J, faculty mtg) all remind me God is real, I can remember when faith shaken or situations occur

Related scriptures: Exodus 3:1-6; Judges 6:11-24; Acts 9:3-9.

> *And the Lord said, Forasmuch as this people draw near Me with their mouth and honor Me with their lips but remove their hearts and minds far from Me, and **their fear and reverence for Me are a commandment of men that is learned by repetition** [without any thought as to the meaning]...*
>
> —Isaiah 29:13 AMP
> [emphasis added]

G 2. In Isaiah's day and Jesus' day, <u>many people served God out of *routine*</u>. Their <u>heart was not in</u> it; their faith was not based on the true fear of the Lord. Therefore, their image of Him was greatly diminished. The same thing can happen to us today—we can have a *form of godliness* but deny its power (see 2 Timothy 3:5).

God's Glory | 45

a. Read Isaiah 29:13 and, in your own words, explain what it means to serve God out of routine.

Rick - repeat certain prayers or Scripture mechanically w/out thought of what you're saying

b. What causes you to fall into a rut of routine in your relationship with God—what steals the joy and life of your salvation?

Rick - rush of going to & fro / distractions of life: TV, computer, etc.

Nan - getting too busy

c. What practical steps can you take to continually cultivate intimacy with the Lord?

Rick - pray diligently & often

> ## Declaring His Greatness
>
> "In the beginning, God made man in His image. Man has been making God in his image ever since. Call it naturalism. Call it anthropomorphism. Call it idolatry. Call it what you will. The result of this spiritual inversion is a god who is about our size and looks an awful lot like us. And most of our spiritual shortcomings stem from this fundamental mistake: thinking about God in human terms. We make God in our image, and as A.W. Tozer said in *The Knowledge of the Holy*, we're left with a god who 'can never surprise us, never overwhelm us, nor astonish us, nor transcend us.'"
>
> —Mark Batterson[1]

You shall have no other gods before or besides Me. You shall not make yourself any graven image [to worship it] or any likeness of anything that is in the heavens above, or that is in the earth beneath, or that is in the water under the earth; you shall not bow down yourself to them or serve them.

—Exodus 20:3-5 AMP
[emphasis added]

3. People who are *not* actively pursuing a relationship with God often lack an accurate image of who He is. Consequently, they tend to develop their own "graven" image of Him, connecting Him to things they are familiar with in the world. This is what the Israelites did when they created the golden calf and worshiped it as the "God who led them out of Egypt."

   a. What kinds of problems arise when we reduce God's image of greatness to someone like us? Have you experienced this in your own life? If so, what did you learn?

   Nan + Rick - we put Him in a box & limit Him in our minds.

   Nan - put God in box re healing, thereby limiting His abil. to work in my life

   b. *Get quiet before the Lord.* Ask Him to reveal any "gods" you may have created and served above Him. Take some time to repent and praise Him for greater revelation of who He truly is.

   Rick - acquiring things, possessions

   Nan - possessions, having to do, games

   c. What are some of the benefits of magnifying the Lord and allowing Him to be the indescribable, uncontainable, and immeasurable God that He is? What are some practical, simple ways to do this?

   Rick - less worry //

   Nan - more trust // prayer + praise + sing

> *Oh, magnify the Lord with me, and let us exalt His name together.*
>
> —Psalm 34:3 NKJV
> [emphasis added]

GOD'S GLORY | 47

[G] 4 Understanding the names of God is a great way to enlarge your vision of who He is and expand your expectations of His greatness in your life. He has numerous names throughout the Bible that describe His immense, unchanging character. Here are just a few:

NAME OF THE LORD	HEBREW MEANING	EXAMPLE IN SCRIPTURE
Jehovah-Jireh	"The Lord Will Provide"	Genesis 22:14
Jehovah-Nissi	"The Lord My Banner"	Exodus 17:15
Jehovah-Shalom	"The Lord My Peace"	Judges 6:24
Jehovah-Tsidkenu	"The Lord Our Righteousness"	Jeremiah 23:6; 33:16
Jehovah-Shammah	"The Lord Is There"	Ezekiel 48:35
Jehovah-Mekaddesh	"The Lord Who Sanctifies"	Exodus 31:13; Leviticus 21:8, 15, 23
El Shaddai	"The Lord Almighty" (The God of More Than Enough)	Genesis 17:1; 35:11 Psalm 91:1

a. How does meditating on the names of the Lord enlarge your perspective of who He is?

Rick - He is many things, wears many hats - break Him down to many facets
Nancy - brings to mind His greatness - enlarges Him to me

b. Which name stirs up the most faith and encouragement in you? Why is it so special?

El-Shaddai - indicates His power - no one greater

c. God promises special blessings to those who acknowledge, know, and trust in His name. Check out Psalm 91:14-16 to see what they are.

blessings = rescue, protect, answer when he prays, be w/ in trouble, deliver, honor, satisfy w/ long life, show him salvation

> *To the only wise God be glory forever through Jesus Christ! Amen.*
>
> —Romans 16:27 NIV

Declaring His Greatness

"You and I both have ideas, images of God that are untrue, which the Holy Spirit would remove if we would let Him. These are cultural and doctrinal traditions which have become ingrained in our minds. The power of Christ's life is filtered and proportionally diminished by the number of these wrong images existing within us. Individuals, churches and even nationalities superimpose their likenesses upon our concepts of God. Poor and rich nations alike suppose that the Almighty Creator exists and thinks as they do. They are not serving God but the *image* they have of God. Yet, the Living One is not a Caucasian or a Negro. He is not a Greek or Jew, a Catholic or a Protestant. He is God!"

—Francis Frangipane[2]

5 **G** One way that we sometimes diminish God's glory and reduce His image of greatness is by *acting as if He doesn't see our attitudes or actions*. That's what the leaders of Israel did during the time of Ezekiel (see Ezekiel 8:12). The fear of the Lord protects us from this.

a. Have you ever said to yourself, *God doesn't see what I'm doing,* or *I'm going to do this, and then ask God to forgive me*? If so, what was it about, and why is this attitude dangerous?

It leads to sin which leads to destruction – eternal fire —
Rick – procrastinate – hide from God

N.– put off what need to do vs want to – food – maybe God will forgive

Consider Romans 6:14-18; Jude 3-7.

b. As of this moment, are you attempting to hide anything from God? If so, what is it?

Appeal to God's merciful, forgiving nature and repent. The fear of the Lord will help you stay clean inside and out!

GOD'S GLORY | 49

You can't keep your true self hidden forever; before long you'll be exposed. You can't hide behind a religious mask forever; sooner or later the mask will slip and your true face will be known. You can't whisper one thing in private and preach the opposite in public; the day's coming when those whispers will be repeated.

—Luke 12:2-3 The Message

6 God says a number of things in His Word about trying to hide things from Him and why it is futile. Read these scriptures and write what the Holy Spirit reveals to you.

> For the ways of man are directly before the eyes of the Lord, and He [Who would have us live soberly, chastely, and godly] carefully weighs all man's goings.
>
> —Proverbs 5:21 AMP

> The eyes of the Lord are in every place, keeping watch on the evil and the good.
>
> —Proverbs 15:3 NKJV

> For God watches how people live; he sees everything they do.
>
> —Job 34:21 NLT

> I can see everything you are doing, even if you try to hide your sins from me.
>
> —Jeremiah 16:17 CEV

What is the Lord showing you in these verses about trying to hide things from Him? How are you challenged and encouraged?

Rick - It's futile to hide // I'm challenged to straighten up + fly rt; He sees others too

Now - commit to a plan, be disciplined to carry it out

> "You can't hide anything from God, but you would be amazed at how many people try. When you walk in the conscious awareness of the fear of the Lord, you know that nothing is hidden from Him. Everything—every motive, every intention, every deed lies open before Him because He is not a man."
>
> JOHN BEVERE

7 Having a healthy fear of the Lord protects us from thinking He doesn't see our actions or our attitudes. It empowers us to remember that we will one day stand before Him and give an account for the life we have lived.

Meditate on the Message

So we make it our goal to please him, whether we are at home in the body or away from it. For we must all appear before the judgment seat of Christ, that each one may receive what is due him for the things done while in the body, whether good or bad. Since, then, we know what it is to fear the Lord, we try to persuade men.

—2 Corinthians 5:9-11 NIV

There is nothing that can be hid from God; everything in all creation is exposed and lies open before his eyes. And it is to him that we must all give an account of ourselves.

—Hebrews 4:13 TEV

The last and final word is this: Fear God. Do what he tells you. And that's it. Eventually God will bring everything that we do out into the open and judge it according to its hidden intent, whether it's good or evil.

—Ecclesiastes 12:13-14 The Message

a. What positive perspective can you develop from these passages and Matthew 6:1-7?

Rick - to pray + do good deeds in secret for God, not man

b. How do they motivate you to live to please the Lord? What changes, if any, is the Lord prompting you to make in your life?

Rick -

Nan - put my desire to please God at the forefront each day

G 8 One of the greatest blessings of having the fear of the Lord is having a desire *not* to sin. As your godly fear grows, your desire to sin diminishes. This is why Moses told the Israelites, "Don't be afraid. God has come to test you and instill a deep and reverent awe [*fear*] within you so that you won't sin" (Exodus 20:20 The Message, emphasis added).

a. What has been your mindset toward sin up to this point? Have you avoided sin simply because you know it's wrong, or have you avoided it because of your fear and love of the Lord—having a desire *not* to sin?

Rick - mostly cause it's wrong

Nan -

> ## Declaring
> # HIS GREATNESS
>
> "New Covenant fear of God is heaven's antidote against casualness toward once-besetting sins. The Holy Ghost-given fear is the open door to supernatural peace and strength. The precious fear of God prepares the heart to receive every other covenant blessing. ....What exactly does it mean to walk in the fear of the Lord? In short, it means reminding yourself of his warnings. And it means allowing the Holy Ghost to bring your sins out into the open for you to acknowledge and cast them far away from you."
>
> —*David Wilkerson*[3]

b. What consequences of sin can you **avoid** by having a healthy fear of the Lord?

God listens when you pray, listens when you do His will, God protects you when you're doing what's right

Check out Psalm 66:16-20; Isaiah 59:1-2; John 9:31; Joshua 7:11-12.

> *Unfailing love and faithfulness make atonement for sin. By fearing the Lord, people avoid evil.*
>
> —Proverbs 16:6 NLT

> "The root of all sin and disobedience is a lack of the fear of the Lord. The fear of the Lord keeps us from sinning. It draws us toward God intimately. Oh, how freeing and liberating the fear of the Lord is!"
>
> **JOHN BEVERE**

9. If your fear of God is based on your image of Him, how can you develop a pure, clear, accurate image of God? By fixing your eyes on Jesus, His Son. Remember what Jesus said, "Anyone who has seen Me has seen the Father" (John 14:9 AMP).

Meditate on the Message

> No one has ever seen God. The only Son, who is truly God and is closest to the Father, has shown us what God is like.
>
> —John 1:18 CEV

> {*Jesus said*} "Whoever looks at me is looking, in fact, at the One who sent me."
>
> —John 12:45 The Message

> Christ is the visible image of the invisible God. He existed before anything was created and is supreme over all creation.
>
> —Colossians 1:15 NLT

Declaring HIS GREATNESS

"Jesus, the incomparable Son of God, is the One through Whom the Father has manifest *all* His glory, fullness, purpose and power. …He is the composite of the [Light] spectrum of God's Fullness. Through Him every facet of the fullness of the Godhead has been unfolded to mankind. Ours is to receive the full revelation of all His work and wonders. Ours is to be enfolded by the glorious spectrum of His manifestations. As Jesus Himself is the prism through Whom we have seen the glory of God, His full Person and works are the spread of divine color which is needed to brighten the world today."

—*Jack Hayford*[4]

[word in brackets added for clarity]

He {*Jesus*} is the sole expression of the glory of God [the Light-being, the out-raying or radiance of the divine], and He is the perfect imprint and very image of [God's] nature.

—*Hebrews 1:3* AMP

{*Unbelievers are*} ...stone-blind to the dayspring brightness of the Message that shines with Christ, who gives us the best picture of God we'll ever get.

—*2 Corinthians 4:4* The Message
[emphasis added]

Get quiet before the Lord. What words surface that describe the character of Christ? Jot them down. Then, ask the Holy Spirit to reveal Jesus to you like you've never seen or known Him before.

_____
_____
_____
_____
_____
_____
_____
_____
_____
_____

Keep your eyes on Jesus, who both began and finished this race we're in. Study how he did it. Because he never lost sight of where he was headed—that exhilarating finish in and with God—he could put up with anything along the way: Cross, shame, whatever. And now he's there, in the place of honor, right alongside God. When you find yourselves flagging in your faith, go over that story again, item by item, that long litany of hostility he plowed through. That will shoot adrenaline into your souls!

—Hebrews 12:2-3 The Message
[emphasis added]

The Blessings of Fearing God

He will bless those who fear the Lord, from the least important to the most important. May the Lord continue to bless you and your children. You will be blessed by the Lord, the maker of heaven and earth.
—*Psalm 115:13-15* GW

Better a little with the fear of the Lord than great wealth with turmoil. Better a meal of vegetables where there is love than a fattened calf with hatred.
—*Proverbs 15:16-17* NIV

Fear the Lord, you his godly people, for those who fear him will have all they need. Even strong young lions sometimes go hungry, but those who trust in the Lord will lack no good thing.
—*Psalm 34:9-10* NLT

Weekly Activity 3

Right Where You Live
WHAT WOULD YOU CHANGE?

Imagine, for a moment, that Jesus Christ, in all of His radiant glory, is standing right beside you, walking with you everywhere you go. What things would you change? What would you do differently?

- What movies would you choose not to go see at the theater or rent to watch at home? Are there any you own that you would throw away?

  _____
  _____
  _____
  _____

- What music would you choose not to listen to? Are there any CDs you would get rid of?

  _____
  _____

God's Glory | 55

- What TV and radio shows would you choose to turn off and no longer watch/listen to?

- What Internet sites would you choose to not visit anymore?

- Who would you choose to no longer spend time with?

- How would you choose to speak differently to other people—especially your children, spouse and parents?

- How would you choose to spend your time differently? What would you stop doing—what would you *start* doing?

- How would you choose to spend your money differently?

- Are there any other activities or habits that you would choose to stop or start? If so, which ones?

_____
_____
_____

As a born-again believer, Jesus lives *inside* of you. Therefore, He **is** with you everywhere you go, listening to everything you say, observing all of the media you are feeding on, spending time with everyone you spend time with, etc. So, be mindful of His presence—allow His loving Spirit to guide you and the fear of the Lord to protect you from evil.

Weekly Devotional 3 | THE BEAUTY OF HOLINESS

> *Give to the Lord the glory due His name; bring an offering, and come before Him. Oh, worship the Lord in the **beauty of holiness**! Tremble before Him, all the earth.*
>
> —1 Chronicles 16:29-30 NKJV
> [emphasis added]

Without question, the greatest characteristic of God's image is His **holiness**. And His holiness is inseparably infused into every aspect of who He is and what He does. Just think of the adjective most frequently used throughout Scripture to describe Him—*holy*. Verse after verse resounds His glory with accolades like, "Praise His *holy* name," "Ascending His *holy* hill," "Standing on *holy* ground," "Enter the Most *Holy* Place," "Proclaim His *holy* Word," and on and on it goes.

So, what does it mean to be *holy*?
Separated *from* sin and separated *to* God—that is what it means to be holy as a believer. Holiness literally means "moral wholeness."[5] The words *holiness* and *sanctification* are from the same Greek word *hagiasmos*, and therefore have the same meaning. To be holy is to be sanctified—separated from sin and separated to God for His use.[6]

In Hebrew, the words for holy are *qados, qadas,* and *qodes*, which basically mean "pure, devoted," and "to sanctify." Just as in Greek, the Hebrew words for "holy" and "holiness" are synonymous with the words "sanctify" and "sanctification." A person or thing that was said to be holy was "set aside (consecrated—usually exclusively) for use in the worship of God."[7]

The Israelites were called God's *holy* people by virtue of being a descendant of Abraham. God had selected them as His own. Similarly, as a Christian, you are holy by virtue of being *in Christ*. This is your position in the Spirit. The moment you repent of your sins and invite Jesus into your heart as Savior and Lord, your spirit is born again and made holy. This is justification—it's *just-as-if* you never sinned. This is what God means when He says, "If anyone is in Christ, he is a new creation; the old has gone, the new has come!" (2 Corinthians 5:17 NIV).

Thankfully, God doesn't stop there. What He starts in our spirit, He continues in our soul, which is basically our mind, will, and emotions. While justification is an instantaneous regeneration of our spirit, sanctification is a lifelong *process* that regenerates our soul. Through our intimate relationship with the Lord, what *we* want, think, and feel is changed to reflect what *He* wants, thinks, and feels. God's part in the process is to give us the *power* and *desire* to change. Our part is to yield our will to His, one choice at a time. God will not do our part, and we cannot do His.

Meditate on the Message
Now may the God of peace make you holy in every way, and may your whole spirit and soul and body be kept blameless until our Lord Jesus Christ comes again. God will make this happen, for he who calls you is faithful.

—*1 Thessalonians* 5:23-24 NLT

God is the one who began this good work in you, and I am certain that he won't stop before it is complete on the day that Christ Jesus returns.

—*Philippians* 1:6 CEV

As for us, we can't help but thank God for you, dear brothers and sisters loved by the Lord. We are always thankful that God chose you to be among the first to experience salvation—a salvation that came through the Spirit who makes you holy and through your belief in the truth.

—*2 Thessalonians* 2:13 NLT

Related scriptures: Philippians 2:12-13; Hebrews 13:20-21; 1 Peter 1:2.

What principle regarding being made holy (sanctified) is repeated in these scriptures?

What else is the Holy Spirit showing you through these encouraging verses?

Bob Sorge, a dynamic author empowering believers in their relationship with Christ, brings clarity and simplicity to the topic of holiness in his book *Secrets of the Secret Place*. He writes...

> "Holiness is not an inherent quality we carry; it is a derived quality that we take on. Holiness has but one source, the Holy One. *Holiness has to do with proximity to the throne.* The seraphim are called 'holy ones,' not because of *who* they are but because of *where* they are. They are 'holy ones' because they live in the immediate presence of the Holy One! I am holy only to the extent that I abide in His holy presence.
>
> I used to define holiness more by what we *don't* do, but now I define it more by what we *do* do. Holiness is found in drawing near to the holy flame of the Trinity. There, anything unholy is burned like stubble, and all that is holy is enflamed and made hotter.
>
> ...Holy men live in the presence of the Holy Spirit. Once you've known this intimacy, you realize that nothing is worth losing it! Holiness is much more than simply clean living. *Holiness is a life lived before the throne of God.*"[8]

Reread the excerpt.

What connection can you see between becoming holy and having an intimate relationship with the Lord?

GOD'S GLORY | 59

What other insights is the Holy Spirit showing you in this excerpt?

_____
_____
_____
_____

Accompanied by the Holy Spirit, there is one more indispensable gift God has given us to make us holy. It is His wonderful Word. The Word not only gives us an accurate image of who God is, it also gives us an accurate image of who we are in Christ. Read these verses and write what the Holy Spirit reveals to you about how He uses God's Word to make you holy.

John 17:17; Ephesians 5:26; James 1:21 • John 14:26; 16:13-15; 1 John 2:27

_____
_____
_____
_____
_____
_____

Clearly, it is the work of the **Holy** Spirit living in you that makes you *holy*. Be ready and willing to work with Him. Regularly feed on God's Word and put it into practice. Yield your will to His. As you live in His presence and agree to His promptings, He will make you holy! (See Hebrews 12:10.)

My Journal
THINGS I WANT TO REMEMBER

Hopefully you can see how important your image of God is and how that determines your ability to fear the Lord. Through the blessing of the fear of the Lord, you have the hope of seeing His glorious image reproduced in your life. Would you like a renewed vision of who God is? Pray this prayer from your heart:

Prayer for renewed vision

Father, please forgive me for creating any false images of You in my mind. Remove them by the power of Your Holy Spirit. Create on the canvas of my heart the true image of who You are! Give me the desire and grace [strength, ability, and power] *to feed on Your Word and stay in Your presence. I want my relationship with You to always be fresh and life-giving. I love You, Lord. Thank you for hearing and answering my prayer...in Jesus' name, amen.*

Take some time to quietly reflect upon and write down anything the Holy Spirit is revealing.

[Handwritten notes:]

4-7-11

Word: Holiness — Order, Glory, Greatness
fear — glory of God - splendor, magnificence
mercy, love — Rev. 22 - bring us into His Glory
worship — divine order → glory → blessings
salvation — (any irreverence = judgment)
praise, thank — Ps 8:5 - Crown man w/ glory
dreams — Lev. 10:3

temple finished (divine order) → priests sanctified → 120 as 1 → (glory) → blessing + prosperity (judgment)

1) John Baptist - begin gospel of J - repentance so in order — level playing field

---

CHAPTER OVERVIEW

Those who fear the Lord are blessed with the ability to recognize Him and see His glory. If your fear of God decreases, His glory decreases. On the contrary, when your fear of God *increases*, His glory *increases* in and through your life. So, keep the fire of the fear of the Lord burning brightly in your heart by staying in His Word and His presence. As you continue to fix your eyes on Jesus, the image of who God is will become clearer and His glory will manifest more and more!

---

(1) Mark Batterson, *Wild Goose Chase* (Colorado Springs, CO: Multnomah Books, 2008) p. 71. (2) Francis Frangipane, *Holiness, Truth and the Presence of God* (Cedar Rapids, IA: Arrow Publications, 1999) p. 84. (3) David Wilkerson, The *New Covenant Unveiled* (Lindale, TX: Wilkerson Trust Publications, 2000) pp. 76-77. (4) Jack Hayford, *A Passion for Fullness* (Dallas, TX; Word Publishing, 1990) pp. 74-75. (5) Adapted from *The New Unger's Bible Dictionary*, Merrill F. Unger (Chicago, IL: Moody Press, Revised and Updated Edition 1988). (6) Adapted from *Vine's Complete Expository Dictionary of Old and New Testament Words*, W. E. Vine (Nashville, TN: Thomas Nelson, Inc. 1996) pp. 307, 545 NT. (7) Ibid., pp. 113-114; 210-213. (8) Bob Sorge, *Secrets of the Secret Place* (Lee's Summit, MO: Oasis House, 2001) pp. 136-137.

My Notes

2) Jesus - lay foundation of Church
3) sacrifice of J
4) Glory - pentecost (120 peop in house)

*By those who come near Me
I must be regarded as holy; and before
all the people I must be glorified.*

—*Leviticus 10:3* NKJV
[emphasis added]

ORDER, GLORY, JUDGMENT

Please refer to session 4 of the teaching series, along with chapters 4, 5 and 6 in *The Fear of the Lord* book.

GLORY

The Hebrew word for "glory" ... is defined as "<u>the weight of something, but only figuratively in a good sense</u>." Its definition also speaks of splendor, abundance, and honor.[1]

And he said, "Please, show me Your glory."

—Exodus 33:18 NKJV

I have looked for You...to see Your power and Your glory.

—Psalm 63:2 NKJV

G 1 Just like Moses, David and Paul, our heart's cry should be to see the glory of the Lord. What does your pursuit of His glory look like? How do you currently understand and comprehend His glory?

Rick - shining, bright light that radiates from His presence

Nancy - Radiating presence + what He creates that reflects that glory

> "There is a pattern occurring throughout the Old and New Testaments. The pattern is: *divine order, God's glory, judgment.* Before God manifests His glory, there must be divine order. Once His glory is revealed, there is great blessing. But once His glory is revealed, any irreverence, disorder, or disobedience is met with immediate judgment."
>
> JOHN BEVERE

[G] 2. In the beginning, God created the heavens and the earth. Within six days, He brought divine order out of chaos through the power of His spoken Word. With each step of the earth's preparation, He released His glory into it—man being the apex of His creation.

   a. According to Genesis 1:1-27, the two indispensable ingredients needed to bring order out of chaos are God's Word and His Spirit. What does this say to you about your relationship with Him and having order in your life? *Live by Word of God; do by HS*
   Rick - We must communicate w/ God to have order in our lives
   Nancy - We should live by His Word + operate thru His Spirit

   Consider Zechariah 4:6; Deuteronomy 8:3.

   b. Think... What would have happened if God would have created all the land animals on day two *before* He created the vegetation? Or if He would have created man on day three *before* He created the sun and stars and planted the Garden of Eden?
   the animals + man would have starved, died

c. First Corinthians 14:40 (NKJV) says, "Let all things be done decently and in order." This is what God did during creation. Why do you think order is so important?

It makes things work better my order

3. God instructed Moses and King Solomon in great detail how to build the tabernacle and the temple for Him to dwell in. Once these sanctuaries were completed and *order* was established, He filled them with His glory.

a. Has God been prompting and instructing you to do something in preparation for the days ahead? If so, describe what it is.

Rick - call

Nancy - order in house - place for everything - so can move on to living in home

b. What can you expect Him to do once you obediently carry out His instruction?

Rick -

Nancy - bring His glory in!

c. Is there anything hindering you from moving forward with what God said? If so, what is it? Surrender it to Him in prayer, asking Him for grace (strength) to do all He has asked of you.

Rick -

Nancy - procrastination, laziness

[G] 4 There are a number of parallels between God's glory manifesting on the dedication day of Solomon's Temple and the day of Pentecost. One of the greatest common factors is *unity*, which has everything to do with order. This key component paved the way for God's glory to come.

God's Glory Filling Solomon's Temple
2 Chronicles 5:12-14
120 priests praising God with trumpets
all were in unison, as with one voice
then the temple was filled with God's glory

God's Glory Filling the Temple of Man
Acts 1:15; 2:1-4
120 disciples praising God in prayer
all were in one accord, as one voice to God
then the "temple" of man was filled with God's glory

Meditate on the Message

Dear brothers and sisters, I close my letter with these last words: Be joyful. Grow to maturity. Encourage each other. Live in harmony and peace. Then the God of love and peace will be with you.
—*2 Corinthians 13:11* NLT

Make every effort to keep the unity of the Spirit through the bond of peace (NIV). You were all called to travel on the same road and in the same direction, so stay together, both outwardly and inwardly. You have one Master, one faith, one baptism, one God and Father of all, who rules over all, works through all, and is present in all. Everything you are and think and do is permeated with Oneness.
—*Ephesians 4:3-6* The Message

Finally, all [of you] should be of one and the same mind (united in spirit), sympathizing [with one another], loving [each other] as brethren [of one household], compassionate and courteous (tenderhearted and humble).
—*1 Peter 3:8* AMP

Related scriptures: Philippians 1:27; Colossians 2:2-3.

a. What is the Holy Spirit revealing to you in these verses regarding the need for unity to usher in God's glory once again? What does unity look like on a practical level?

Rick - unity is imp // getting along, loving each other,

Nancy - Unity + order go together - + then God's glory can be shown // unity = agreement, oneness on imp matters

Welcome ov bring in God's glory: order, unity, praise/worship

b. Read Psalm 133 and identify God's promises to you when you pursue unity.

> How wonderful, how beautiful, when brothers and sisters get along! It's like costly *anointing oil* flowing down head and beard, flowing down Aaron's beard, flowing down the collar of his priestly robes. It's like the *dew* on Mount Hermon flowing down the slopes of Zion. Yes, that's where God commands the blessing, ordains eternal life.
> —*Psalm 133* The Message
> [emphasis added]

What do you think the anointing oil represents? How about the dew?

Rick

Nancy — anointing oil = HS - saturating + consecrating
dew — brothers unity

What does God *command* when we pursue unity? How are you experiencing this in your life?

blessing

blessing of family

c. Is there anything you sense the Holy Spirit prompting you to do to promote and cultivate more unity in your marriage, family, church, or workplace? If so, what is it? Ask Him for more ideas!

Rick — having shared goals

Nancy — love husband; allow God to change him — don't demand ov just get along w/ family

5. Another important ingredient that can welcome God's glory is *praise* and *worship*. At the dedication of Solomon's Temple, there were hundreds of singers and musicians who led the people in praise to God. "You are holy, O You Who dwell in [the holy place where] the praises of Israel [are offered]" (Psalm 22:3 AMP).

> ### Declaring
> ## HIS GREATNESS
>
> "Praise *invades hell and excites heaven*! When we praise God, we must think beyond notes, form, or technique. Praise and worship is a powerful expression of love that transcends the possibilities of music. It is given to us as a weapon of warfare or as a warm blanket on a cold night. Praise is a supernatural way of expressing our thanks to our ever-loving God. We must never underestimate the gift and the power of praise and worship."
>
> —Darlene Zschech[2]

Take to heart these instructions to praise and glorify the Lord:

You who fear the Lord, *praise* Him! All you descendants of Jacob, *glorify* Him, and *fear* Him, all you offspring of Israel!

—Psalm 22:23 NKJV

Sing to the Lord! *Give praise* to the Lord! He rescues the life of the needy from the hands of the wicked.

—Jeremiah 20:13 NIV

Shout praises to the Lord! Our God is kind, and it is right and good to sing praises to him.

—Psalm 147:1 CEV
[emphasis added]

Related scriptures: Psalm 135:1-3; 138:1-5; 146:1-2; 149.

a. When you sincerely praise and glorify the Lord, what happens inside of you? How are your thoughts, words, and attitudes affected? Where is your focus?

Rick - focus on God - feel more joyous, serene, hopeful

Nan -

What things seem to silence you from praising God? Surrender these to the Lord in prayer. They are no match for His majesty and strength!

Rick - daily chores, worldly, sleepiness

Nan - distractions, worry, duties taking up time

A great way to ignite a heart of praise is by playing praise and worship music in your home and car. Find some music you really enjoy and let it permeate the atmosphere around you. Joy will fill your heart—thanksgiving and praise will fill your mouth!

b. Write a heartfelt prayer of praise to the Lord. Express your appreciation and love to Him for anything and everything that comes to mind.

My prayer of praise

_____
_____
_____
_____
_____
_____
_____
_____
_____
_____
_____
_____
_____
_____
_____

> ### Declaring HIS GREATNESS
>
> "Many have the idea that they may come to God and worship Him because they have good works which are worthy of His praise. They cannot come and worship if they have not behaved themselves but have done things displeasing to God. Yet we need to understand that our conduct, whether good or bad, has no direct relationship to our approaching God: 'Having therefore, brethren, boldness to enter into the holy place by the blood of Jesus' (Hebrews 10:19). We are told in this verse that our coming to God is based on nothing else than the blood of the Lord Jesus. Neither good works nor zeal nor spiritual experience qualifies us to approach God. The blood of the Lord Jesus alone enables us to draw near to Him."
>
> —*Watchman Nee*[3]

GIVE GOD GLORY!

What does it mean to "give God glory" or "glorify" God? To glorify God means "to magnify, praise, celebrate, and honor Him, acknowledging Him for who He is and what He has done. This includes praise for His incredible characteristics as well as all the wonderful deeds He has done in your life and in the world.[4] We do this with the words of our lips and the actions of our lives.

6. Seeing God bring victory in your difficult situations is definitely a manifestation of His glory. Read how praise and worship paved the way for God's glory to show up for King Jehoshaphat and the people of Judah in 2 Chronicles 20:21-30.

   a. When God heard the praise of the people, what did He do?
   He set ambushes & had Ammon & Moab destroyed Mt Seir, then turned on each other & everyone was killed

   b. What did Jehoshaphat and the people of Judah do after God gave them victory?
   Gathered spoils, returned to Jerusalem & went to the temple & joyfully praised the Lord

   c. What is the Lord showing you in this example? How can you apply it to your life?
   When trials & troubles come, praise God for who He is, awesomeness, put our focus on Him, not our trouble.

7. There is one more indispensable element that opens the door for God's glory to invade earth and that is a *blood sacrifice.* Under the Old Covenant, God ordained the Levites to serve as priests and offer animal sacrifices to cover people's sin. Under the New Covenant, Jesus Christ became our High Priest and the sacrifice to end all sacrifices—the Lamb of God who takes away the sin of the world.

   a. Why is the shedding of blood (sacrifice) necessary?
   Check out: Hebrews 9:16-22 • Leviticus 17:11
   for forgiveness, cleansing of sin

ORDER, GLORY, JUDGMENT | 71

b. How is Jesus' blood *superior* to the blood of animals? What does it do for you?
Check out: Hebrews 9:12-14; 13:12 • 1 Peter 1:18-19 • 1 John 1:7 • Revelation 1:5

cleanses, frees, atones for our sin

c. Read the story of Jesus' sacrifice, paying close attention to what He endured for you. How does reading these passages stir your heart with gratefulness for Him?
Matthew 26:57-75 • Isaiah 50:6; 53:3-7

He took all on His back & didn't say a word. I'm grateful beyond words.

The greatest price that could ever be paid was paid for our sins—the spotless Son of God gave His life for us. Through His costly death and glorious resurrection, He made a way for God's glory to be poured into us. Let His sacrifice be a constant reminder of the value of His glory and your value to Him.

Think About It

In the Old Testament times, God established a system of animal sacrifices by which the people would have their sins atoned for and remain in right relationship with Him. There were several different types of offerings, including one for sin, guilt, and peace as well as a grain and drink offering, a heave and wave offering, a burnt offering, and the red heifer. Sacrificial offerings were made *year round*—during the seven special feasts, *monthly* when the new moon appeared, *weekly* on the Sabbath, and *daily*. A burnt offering was made twice daily—once in the morning and once in the evening (see Numbers 28:3-8). The animal was totally consumed by the flames, symbolizing the entire surrender, and consequently sanctification, of an individual or group. The purpose of the burnt offering was solely to maintain the covenant with Jehovah.[5]

Today, under the new covenant, we no longer have to sacrifice animals. Our awesome Savior, Jesus Christ, became the sacrifice to end all sacrifices (see Hebrews 9:11-28). He gave His life that we might have life. How can we benefit from what He did? Through prayers of *repentance* and *confession of sin* (see 1 John 1:9). Just as our blood circulates in our body every 23.5 seconds to bring nourishment and remove impurities and disease, having a repentant heart keeps the blood of Jesus circulating (spiritually) through our lives. It brings nourishment to our spirit and takes away the disease of sin from our soul! What an awesome God we serve!

> ### IRREVERENT • PROFANE • SCOFFING
> To be *irreverent* is to be disrespectful, mocking, rude, flippant, blasphemous, or profane. The words *irreverent* and *profane* are synonymous. To *scoff* means to: mock, ridicule, laugh at, jeer, or sneer. A person who is irreverent or profane shows disrespect for, or treats as common, things that are holy and precious to the Lord.

[G] 8. Nadab and Abihu were Aaron's sons, Moses' nephews. They were God's anointed and chosen leaders. Yet, they became too familiar with God and His presence and lost their fear of Him. In pride, they second-guessed His instruction on how to bring Him incense and did things *their* way (see Leviticus 10:1-2). As a result, they were swiftly judged.

a. Have you ever treated the Lord as *common* or come into His presence irreverently? Have you ever second-guessed what He told you to do? If so, how?

Nan — I'm sure I have // lots of times

b. What can you choose to focus on to keep God's greatness alive in your heart and remain in right relationship with Him?

Rick — focus on Jesus

c. What is the Holy Spirit communicating to you through Nadab and Abihu's example?

Rick — Its imp. how we approach the L.

Nan — I need to do things God's way. Treat holy what He treats holy.

9. Today, under the New Covenant, God inhabits the hearts of people—the way He desired to be in relationship with us from the beginning. Everyone who believes in and receives Christ into their heart becomes a *temple of the Holy Spirit* to dwell in. What an amazing privilege and responsibility!

> ### Meditate on the Message
> Don't you realize that your body is the temple of the Holy Spirit, who lives in you and was given to you by God? You do not belong to yourself, for God bought you with a high price. So you must honor God with your body.
> —*1 Corinthians 6:19-20* NLT

Who would think of setting up pagan idols in God's holy Temple? But that is exactly what we are, each of us a temple in whom God lives. God himself put it this way: "I'll live in them, move into them; I'll be their God and they'll be my people. So leave the corruption and compromise; leave it for good," says God. "Don't link up with those who will pollute you. I want you all for myself. I'll be a Father to you; you'll be sons and daughters to me." The Word of the Master, God.

—*2 Corinthians 6:16-18* The Message

Declaring HIS GREATNESS

"Without question, the teaching of the New Testament is that the very God Himself inhabits the nature of His true children. How this can be I do not know, but neither do I know how my soul inhabits my body. Paul called this wonder of the indwelling God a rich mystery: 'Christ in you, the hope of glory.' …What kind of habitation pleases God? What must our natures be like before He can feel at home within us? He asks nothing but a pure heart and a single mind. He asks no rich paneling, no rugs from the Orient, no art treasures from afar. He desires but sincerity, transparency, humility and love. He will see to the rest."

—*A.W. Tozer*[6]

And so, dear brothers and sisters, I plead with you to give your bodies to God because of all he has done for you. Let them be a living and holy sacrifice—the kind he will find acceptable. This is truly the way to worship him.

—*Romans 12:1* NLT

a. How do these verses challenge the way you are caring for your body (God's temple)? Examine all areas—not only the way you are nourishing your physical body, but also your soul and spirit.

Rick - overemphasize physical over soul + spirit need to praise, pray & talk to HS more

Nan - I need to take better care of it.

b. Is God prompting you to do any "remodeling"? If so, what is He asking you to do?

Rick - praise, pray, talk to HS more

Nan - eat better, ex // pray, study Bible, praise

> "I want to challenge you before you pray to really do what Jesus said in the Lord's Prayer. Take time to meditate on the awesomeness of the Father you are calling on. Say, 'Our Father, who art in heaven, Hallowed be thy name.' He is your Father, but He is also a consuming fire."
>
> JOHN BEVERE

Do you see what we've got? An unshakable kingdom! And do you see how thankful we must be? Not only thankful, but brimming with worship, deeply reverent before God. For God is not an indifferent bystander. He's actively cleaning house, torching all that needs to burn, and he won't quit until it's all cleansed. **God himself is Fire!**

—Hebrews 12:28-29 The Message
[emphasis added]

10. The glory of the Lord is truly awe-inspiring! Scripture says He is a *consuming fire*.[7] In the Old Testament times, the *fire* of God dwelled in the Tabernacle

Order, Glory, Judgment | 75

and the Temple. Under the New Covenant, the *fire* of God dwells *within* the spirit of man—a phenomenon that first took place on the day of Pentecost.

> ### Declaring
> ### HIS GREATNESS
> "Each one of us has a FIRE in our heart for something. It's our goal in life to find it and keep it lit."
> —Mary Lou Retton⁸

a. Think about it. What positive things can you think of that fire does? How might these things relate to the fire of God in you?

Positive attributes of fire	What this means spiritually
supplies light	light for direction
warms things up	passion
cooks food	makes palatable
burns up garbage	burns dross
supplies energy →	
does work	God does work in ea of us

b. *Meditate on the Message* of these verses and write what they communicate to you.

> The spirit of man is the *lamp* of the Lord, searching all the innermost parts of his being.
> —Proverbs 20:27 NASB

> For *You light my lamp*; the Lord my God illumines my darkness.
> —Psalm 18:28 NASB
> [emphasis added]

if you have Spirit in your heart

Nan - God lights my darkness

While John baptized with water, Jesus baptizes us with His Holy Spirit and fire (see Matthew 3:11). Have you received this amazing expression of God's presence? He stands ready and willing to give you this gift; all you need to do is ask. Jesus said, "Which one of you fathers would give your hungry child a snake if the child asked for a fish? Which one of you would give your child a scorpion if the child asked for an egg? As bad as you are, you still know how to give good gifts to your children. But *your heavenly Father is even more ready to give the Holy Spirit to anyone who asks*" (Luke 11:11-13 CEV, emphasis added).

Once you ask for the Holy Spirit, you will *receive* the Holy Spirit. Acts 2:4 says, "And they were all filled with the Holy Spirit and began to speak with other tongues, as the Spirit gave them utterance" (NKJV). The word *utterance* means "syllables, sounds or words." After you pray, you will probably sense a syllable, sound or word bubbling up inside of your spirit or swirling around in your head. Although the impression may be faint and you may feel silly, SPEAK IT OUT! That's the Holy Spirit. He is giving you the utterance, but you must YIELD your lips, tongue and vocal chords to speak what He is impressing on you.

If you desire this dynamic gift of God's Spirit, pray this prayer from your heart, believing you will have what you ask for.

> *Father, I come to You in the name of Jesus, asking You for the gift of Your Holy Spirit. Please forgive me of any sin that would keep me from receiving; wash me clean with the blood of Jesus. If I am holding on to unforgiveness toward anyone, I choose to release them and bless them.*
>
> *Now, as Your child, I ask You for the promised gift of the Holy Spirit. Jesus said if I ask You for the Holy Spirit, You would give Him to me. I can't be good enough to earn Him; all You require me to do is ask. Please baptize me with Your Holy Spirit and fire. I receive everything You have for me, including the ability to speak in a new language like they did in the book of Acts. Now by faith I receive Him and believe Your glory will begin manifesting in and through my life in new ways...in Jesus' name, amen!*

Take some time to express your experience and anything He spoke to your heart.

Declaring His Greatness

"The Lord wants all saved people to receive power from on High—power to witness, power to act, power to live, and power to show forth the divine manifestation of God within. The power of God will take you out of your own plans and put you into the plan of God. ...Instead of your laboring according to your own plan, it will be God working in you and through you to do His own good pleasure through the power of the Spirit within."

—*Smith Wigglesworth*[9]

The Blessings of Fearing God

Behold, the Lord's eye is upon those who fear Him [who revere and worship Him with awe], who wait for Him and hope in His mercy and loving-kindness, to deliver them from death and keep them alive in famine.

—*Psalm 33:18-19* AMP

In the fear of the Lord there is strong confidence, and His children will have a place of refuge. The fear of the Lord is a fountain of life, to turn one away from the snares of death.

—*Proverbs 14:26-27* NKJV

The fear of the Lord leads to life, and he who has it will abide in satisfaction; he will not be visited with evil.

—*Proverbs 19:23* NKJV

Weekly Activity 4

Right Where You Live
GET READY...COMPANY IS COMING!

...This is what the Lord says: Put your  *....*

—Isaiah 38:1 NIV
[emphasis added]

What do you do when you know company is coming? You get your house in order. You get things ready so that you are *prepared* for the arrival of your special guest. John the Baptist came to prepare the way of the Lord, the greatest guest we could ever welcome into our lives. Read this passage and listen for the voice of God's Spirit crying out to your spirit...

Prepare the way of the Lord!

Make straight in the desert a highway for our God. Every valley shall be exalted and every mountain and hill brought low; the crooked places shall be made straight and the rough places smooth; the glory of the Lord shall be revealed, and all flesh shall see it together; for the mouth of the Lord has spoken.

—*Isaiah 40:3-5* NKJV

IN YOUR LIFE...

- What areas are like a VALLEY that needs to be lifted?
  Are there any areas where you feel lowly, rejected, shameful or condemned?

  Rick - don't want to feel depressed; turn away from L + do it myself ~~doing it myself~~

  Nan - ~~ill _____~~ fear, procrastination

- What areas are like a MOUNTAIN that needs to be brought low?
  Are there any areas where you have pride that need to be replaced with humility?

  Rick - my ego + pride, doing it myself

  Nan - ~~pride is~~ selfishness

- What areas are CROOKED that need to be straightened out?
  Are there any areas where you are not walking in total truth—areas where you have compromised or been deceived?

  Rick - I don't need the L

  Nan - food, gluttony

- What areas are ROUGH that need smoothing out?
  Are there any areas where you are impatient, immature, or need more control?

  Rick - ruts I stay stuck

  Nan - anger

ADMIT you have room to grow in these areas. Humility opens the door for God's mercy and grace.

SUBMIT yourself to the Lord afresh, repenting of any sin and receiving His forgiveness.

COMMIT these areas of your life to Him in prayer and renew your mind with the truth of His Word.

Company is coming! Get ready! Surrender yourself to the Lord and He will help you put your spiritual house in order and prepare the way for a fresh infilling of His glory.

THE GIFT OF REPENTANCE

For godly grief and the pain God is permitted to direct, produce a repentance that leads and contributes to salvation and deliverance from evil, and it never brings regret; but worldly grief (the hopeless sorrow that is characteristic of the pagan world) is deadly [breeding and ending in death].

—2 Corinthians 7:10 AMP
[emphasis added]

There are a number of words that come to mind when thinking of the Christian faith—words like love, mercy, grace, and forgiveness. There is one more word, however, that cannot be omitted. It is a life-giving link that reconnects God and man in right relationship; it is the gift of *repentance*. Repentance is the initial act that brings order to the chaos of our lives. It is also the ongoing act that maintains order. Repentance sums up the entire purpose of John the Baptist's ministry of preparation, a ministry so important it is mentioned in all four gospels: "**Repent of your sins and turn to God, for the Kingdom of Heaven is near**" (Matthew 3:2 NLT, emphasis added).

What is repentance?
Repentance is a change of direction. It is from the Greek word *metanoia*, meaning "a change of mind." True repentance indicates a thorough turning in our heart **from sin** and **toward God**.[10] Jesus' parable of the Prodigal Son is an excellent example of genuine repentance (see Luke 15:11-24).

Repentance is reason for rejoicing. Jesus said, "…there will be more rejoicing in heaven over one sinner who repents than over ninety-nine righteous persons who do not need to repent" (Luke 15:7 NIV). What a gift it is to genuinely repent—to not only admit we did wrong, but also have the desire and power to change our heart and mind to the right direction. It is through God's grace we have that power to repent and live a life of holiness. (See Hebrews 12:28.)

Please realize that admitting we have done wrong and feeling sorry about it is *not* the same thing as true repentance. The Bible is filled with people who confessed their sin but didn't truly repent. Think about it…

Pharaoh said, "I have sinned." (See Exodus 10:16.)

Balaam said, "I have sinned." (See Numbers 22:34.)
Achan said, "I have sinned." (See Joshua 7:20.)
Saul said, "I have sinned." (See 1 Samuel 15:24, 30.)
Judas said, "I have sinned." (See Matthew 27:4.)

Yet, none of these men truly repented. They just made a confession.

WHAT IS CONFESSION?
Confession in the Greek literally means "to speak the same thing." It is from the word *homologeo*. When we confess our sins to God, we get in agreement with Him—we say with Him that what we did was wrong. It is admitting or acknowledging our sin.[11]

Make no mistake; confession is important. It is the starting point of repentance. But, God doesn't want us to stop there. Once we confess our sin, acknowledging and admitting it, He wants us to repent. He gives us the gift of godly sorrow, enabling us to change our mind and heart, *turning from sin* and *toward Him*. Why? Because He loves us and yearns to be in unbroken fellowship.

Read the verses of how David and the prodigal son repented (see Psalm 51; Luke 15:11-24). What elements of genuine repentance can you hear from their heart's cry?

_____
_____
_____
_____
_____
_____

> "If you preach a gospel that is without the baptism of repentance, you get a church that is built on shaky, faulty ground. It has not been made level. As a result, it becomes a 'sign and a byword' that is laughed at and talked about by all generations that follow. That's why we need preachers who will preach not only the good news of the Gospel, but also the requirement of the baptism of repentance."
>
> JOHN BEVERE

Meditate on the Message

If we [freely] admit that we have sinned and *confess* our sins, He is faithful and just (true to His own nature and promises) and will forgive our sins [dismiss our lawlessness] and [continuously] cleanse us from all unrighteousness [everything not in conformity to His will in purpose, thought, and action].

—*1 John 1:9* AMP

And if that nation I warned *repents* of its evil, then I will relent and not inflict on it the disaster I had planned.

—*Jeremiah 18:8* NIV

He who conceals his sins does not prosper, but whoever *confesses* and renounces them finds mercy. Blessed is the man who always *fears the Lord*, but he who hardens his heart falls into trouble.

—*Proverbs 28:13-14* NIV

When I refused to confess my sin, my body wasted away, and I groaned all day long. Day and night your hand of discipline was heavy on me. My strength evaporated like water in the summer heat. Finally, I confessed all my sins to you and stopped trying to hide my guilt. I said to myself, "I will confess my rebellion to the Lord." And you forgave me! All my guilt is gone. Therefore, let all the godly pray to you while there is still time, that they may not drown in the floodwaters of judgment.

—*Psalm 32:3-6* NLT
[emphasis added]

In what ways do you see repentance as a *gift* from God?

Rick - clears your name w/ God

Nan - it restores your relat w/ God

What else is the Lord speaking to you through these verses regarding repentance and confession?

Nan - I need to repent + confess daily

Thank God for His goodness! For that is what leads us to repentance (see Romans 2:4). His Spirit who lives in us *convicts* us of sin, giving us an internal nudge to *confess* and *repent* (see John 16:8). Remember, sin separates; repentance reunites, turning our hearts and minds back to God. Why does He convict us? Why does He tell us to confess our sins and repent? Because He loves us and longs to be in relationship with us. Jesus says, "Those whom I [dearly and tenderly] love, I tell their faults and **convict** and convince and reprove and chasten [I discipline and instruct them]. So be enthusiastic and in earnest and burning with zeal and **repent** [changing your mind and attitude]" (Revelation 3:19 AMP, emphasis added).

Prayer of repentance

Father, thank you for Your mercy, kindness, and patience! Thank you for Your conviction and the gift of repentance. Please forgive me for treating You, Your presence, or sacred things with irreverence. "Purify me from my sins, and I will be clean; wash me, and I will be whiter than snow. Oh, give me back my joy again; You have broken me—now let me rejoice. Don't keep looking at my sins. Remove the stain of my guilt. Create in me a clean heart, O God. Renew a loyal spirit within me. Do not banish me from Your presence, and don't take Your Holy Spirit from me. Restore to me the joy of Your salvation, and make me willing to obey You" (Psalm 51:7-12 NLT). Help me to never become so familiar with You that I treat You as common. I welcome You to make Yourself at home within me, Your temple...in Jesus' name, amen.

My Journal
THINGS I WANT TO REMEMBER

> "You cannot grasp the true fear of the Lord unless you seek to understand how great His glory is. The glory of God is something very important to not only talk about but also to seek. It was Moses' heart cry, David's heart cry, and John's heart cry. It should be our hearts' cry too."
>
> JOHN BEVERE

Order, Glory, Judgment | 83

Has the Holy Spirit opened your eyes to areas of your life that are out of order? If He has, it is because He loves you and wants nothing to stand between you and Him. Take a few moments to share your heart with Him in prayer. Confess any sin, repent by His grace, and receive His loving forgiveness. Remember to write down any new insights He reveals.

CHAPTER OVERVIEW

There is a pattern recurring throughout Scripture in which God brings *divine order, glory*, and then *judgment*. Before God manifests His glory, there must be order. Once His glory is revealed, there is great blessing, but there is also swift judgment for any irreverence or dishonor. While God's glory filled the tabernacle and the temple in the Old Testament times, today His glory fills man himself—the temple of the Holy Spirit. The sacrifice of Jesus Christ makes this manifestation of God's glory possible and reconnects us in right relationship with Him.

---

(1) John Bevere, *The Fear of the Lord* (Lake Mary, FL: Charisma House, A Strang Company, 1997, 2006, 2010) p. 47. (2) Darlene Zschech, *Extravagant Worship* (Bloomington, MN: Bethany House Publishers, 2001, 2002) p. 56. (3) Watchman Nee, *From Faith to Faith* (New York, NY: Christian Fellowship Publishers, Inc., 1984) p. 50. (4) Adapted from Vine's Complete Expository Dictionary of Old and New Testament Words, W. E. Vine (Nashville, TN: Thomas Nelson, Inc. 1996) p. 267, NT. (5) Adapted from *The New Unger's Bible Dictionary*, Merrill F. Unger (Chicago, IL: Moody Press, Revised and Updated Edition 1988) pp. 1102-1109. (6) A.W. Tozer, *A Treasury of A.W. Tozer* (Harrisburg, PA: Christian Publications, Inc., 1980) pp. 133-134. (7) See Exodus 24:17; Deuteronomy 4:24; 9:3; Isaiah 30:27; 33:14; Psalm 50:3; 97:3. (8) Quotes on *Purpose* (http://www.motivational-inspirational-corner.com/getquote.html?startrow=111&categoryid=52, retrieved 9-28-10). (9) Smith Wigglesworth, *Faith That Prevails* (Springfield, MO: Radiant Books, Gospel Publishing House, 1966) p. 38. (10) See note 5, p. 1073. (11) See note 4, p. 120, NT.

My Notes

When a crime is not punished quickly, people feel
it is safe to do wrong. But even though a person
sins a hundred times and still lives a long time,
I know that those who fear God will be better off.
The wicked will not prosper, for they do not fear God.
Their days will never grow long like the evening shadows.

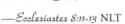

—*Ecclesiastes 8:11-13* NLT

DELAYED JUDGMENT

Please refer to session 5 of the teaching series, along with chapters 7, 8 and 14 in *The Fear of the Lord* book.

> "This truth must be settled in our hearts: The greater God's revealed glory, the greater and swifter the judgment for irreverence! Whenever sin enters the presence of God's glory, there is an immediate reaction. Sin, and anyone who willfully bears it, will be obliterated. The greater the intensity of light, the less chance darkness has to remain."
>
> JOHN BEVERE

G 1 Immediate judgment comes when God's glory is greatly manifesting. Reread John's opening quote along with 1 Samuel 3:1-14, which gives a snapshot of the conditions in Israel under the leadership of Eli the priest.

a. In what ways, if any, do Eli's days and his leadership compare with the current situation in your country?

N- not many visions, Word of Lord is rare

b. Notice the difference between where Eli and Samuel are resting and who hears God's voice. What does this say to you personally?

R- you have to be near God to hear Him.

c. Why has God delayed His judgment for those who are practicing sin yet serving in the church?

R- to give time to repent

X-

> ### Declaring
> ### HIS GREATNESS
>
> "With my whole heart I agree with the psalmist, 'It is time for the Lord to act, for they have broken Thy law' (Psalm 119:126). I believe that if He were to act as decisively as He did so often in biblical times, marvelous changes would sweep across Christendom. A healthy fear of the Lord would again grip His people as respect for His holy name returned. An obedient walk would become evident among us. Furthermore, a renewed determination to uphold one's marital vows would solidify homes. And a purer Bride, with genuine, priceless character, would await the arrival of her Groom."
>
> —*Charles Swindoll*

2. Ananias and Sapphira give us a strong example of why it is imperative to fear the Lord. On the surface, their action of selling a possession and giving part of the proceeds to the Lord seems honorable. But, the true motivation of their hearts revealed otherwise.

a. God was not angry with Ananias and Sapphira because they didn't give all the profits as an offering. What was their true issue of sin?

lying

b. Have you ever done something that on the surface looked honorable, but your true motivation was fleshly (selfish)? If so, what was it? What did you learn from it?

c. How does this New Testament example of God's judgment challenge you and instill godly fear in you?

R - Look at the motivation for your actions; reconsider if not honorable

N - Makes me realize God sees my motivation

> "Let me make an announcement: God hasn't changed. He is the same Holy God that He was in the days of Moses and Aaron. His Word and level of holiness have not varied. God was, is, and will always be the great King, and He must be reverenced as such. We cannot treat what He calls holy lightly."
>
> JOHN BEVERE

3. When Peter corrected Ananias, he told him that he had "not lied to men but to *God*" (Acts 5:4 NKJV, emphasis added). Clearly, God places high importance on being truthful. Jesus Himself *is* the Truth who came into the world to testify to, or give evidence of, the truth (see John 14:6; 18:37).

Meditate on the Message
Truthful words stand the test of time, but lies are soon exposed. The Lord detests lying lips, but he delights in those who tell the truth.
—*Proverbs* 12:19, 22 NLT

What you're after is truth from the inside out. Enter me, then; conceive a new, true life.
—*Psalm* 51:6 The Message

What this adds up to, then, is this: no more lies, no more pretense. Tell your neighbor the truth. In Christ's body we're all connected to each other, after all. When you lie to others, you end up lying to yourself.
—*Ephesians* 4:25 The Message

Related scriptures: Psalm 101:7; Proverbs 23:23; Colossians 3:9.

> ### Declaring
> # HIS GREATNESS
>
> "Any species of designed deception for a selfish reason is *lying*. If you design to make an impression—by words or looks or actions—contrary to the naked truth, God calls it a lie and charges you with lying."
> —Charles Finney[2]

a. What is the Lord showing you in these verses?

Rick — tell the truth

N — The Lord doesn't put up w/ liars

b. Read Psalm 34:11-14. How does it challenge you? How can you apply this truth practically in your life?

R — make sure you're always speaking the truth

N — think before I speak

This truth is so important that Peter repeats it in 1 Peter 3:10-11.

c. Probably the greatest cure for lying is getting a true revelation of the fear of the Lord. Read Matthew 12:35-37. How does it motivate and challenge you to watch what you say?

R — I'll be condemned if I don't speak the truth in peace

N — all my words will be displayed

MOTIVES AND INTENTIONS

The word *motive* means "that which incites to action; that which determines the choice, or moves the will." And the word *intention* signifies "a stretching or bending of the mind towards an object; unwavering attention; a determination to act in a particular manner."[3]

G **4** The things that motivate us to do what we do are our *motives*—they are the "why" behind our every action. Motives are intangible possessions owned by both rich and poor alike. They are continually being birthed in our hearts. The question is, what kind do we have?

> **Meditate on the Message**
> All a man's ways seem innocent to him, but motives are weighed by the Lord.
> —*Proverbs* 16:2 NIV
>
> We justify our actions by appearances; God examines our motives. Clean living before God and justice with our neighbors mean far more to God than religious performance.
> —*Proverbs* 21:2-3 The Message
>
> The human heart is the most deceitful of all things, and desperately wicked. Who really knows how bad it is? But I, the Lord, search all hearts and examine secret motives. I give all people their due rewards, according to what their actions deserve.
> —*Jeremiah* 17:9-10 NLT
>
> My conscience is clear, but that does not make me innocent. It is the Lord who judges me. Therefore judge nothing before the appointed time; wait till the Lord comes. He will bring to light what is hidden in darkness and will expose the motives of men's hearts. At that time each will receive his praise from God.
> —*1 Corinthians* 4:4-5 NIV

Related scriptures: Psalm 26:1-2; 1 Chronicles 28:9; 1 Thessalonians 2:4; James 4:3.

a. God says our hearts are deceitful, making it impossible to know our true motives on our own. So, how can you learn the true motives of your heart?

A- ask God, read the Word

?

Check out Psalm 139:23-24; Hebrews 4:12.

b. When it comes to judging the motives of *others*, what new insights are you seeing?

R—

N— They may not be aware of their motives

c. What else is the Lord speaking to you through these scriptures?

Rick— be careful of motives for they tell where your heart is

N— I can't rely on myself because my heart is deceitful & can decieve even me

Declaring HIS GREATNESS

"There are more than 500 verses in the Bible concerning prayer and nearly 500 verses concerning faith, but more than 2,000 verses on the subject of money and possessions. Jesus talked about money in 16 of His 38 parables. Clearly, from the Bible's standpoint, we need to understand money and how to handle it. Why? Because *money is actually a test from God.* How you handle money reveals volumes about your priorities, loyalties and affections. In fact, it directly dictates many of the blessings you will (or won't) experience in life."

—*Robert Morris*[4]

Scripture says that giving is a *gift* in the body of Christ—a gift that should be recognized and celebrated just like the gifts of teaching and serving (see Romans 12:6-8). But unlike Ananias and Sapphira, we must give with a pure heart.

Meditate on the Message

Let each one [give] as he has made up his own mind and purposed in his heart, not reluctantly or sorrowfully or under compulsion, for God loves (He takes pleasure in, prizes above other things, and is unwilling to abandon or to do without) a cheerful (joyous, "prompt to do it") giver [whose heart is in his giving].

—*2 Corinthians 9:7* AMP

When you give to someone in need, don't do as the hypocrites do—blowing trumpets in the synagogues and streets to call attention to their acts of charity!

Delayed Judgment | 93

I tell you the truth, they have received all the reward they will ever get. But when you give to someone in need, don't let your left hand know what your right hand is doing. Give your gifts in private, and your Father, who sees everything, will reward you.

—Matthew 6:2-4 NLT

Each of you must bring a gift in proportion to the way the Lord your God has blessed you.

—Deuteronomy 16:17 NIV

a. According to these scriptures, **how** are you to give to the Lord and to others? *w/ gladness* *cheerfully, w/ a willing heart, in proportion to how you've been blessed*

b. Does it matter **when** you give to God? What blessings does He promise as you give? *When you get it, when you've been blessed*

Check out Proverbs 3:9; Malachi 3:10-11.

c. What is God's view on generosity? How does it affect the blessing you receive in return? *He blesses (give) more as you bless; sows (gives) generously = reaps generously; generous man will prosper*

Check out Luke 6:38; 2 Corinthians 9:6; Proverbs 11:25.

> "For the past twenty to thirty years, the grace taught and believed in many of our churches is not real grace, but a perversion of it. This is the result of overemphasizing the goodness of God to the neglect of the fear of Him. When the doctrine of the love of God is not balanced with an understanding of the fear of God, error is the result."
>
> **JOHN BEVERE**

[G] 6. The key to being a healthy Christian is learning to *love God* passionately and *fear Him* reverently. This comes from developing a balanced understanding of Him as Abba Father and also Eternal Judge.

a. Read these scriptures describing the Lord as our loving Father. Why is this aspect of His character so important? What else is the Lord showing you in these verses?

John 3:16-18 • Romans 5:8; 8:15 • Ephesians 1:4-6 • Titus 3:3-7

We needed God to reach out to us in love, because we, in sin, couldn't reach Him.
We should honor Him as our father.

b. Examine these verses describing the Lord as Judge. Why is this facet of His character vital? What might life be like *without* it? What else is the Lord revealing to you?

Matthew 25:31-46 • Acts 17:30-31 • 2 Corinthians 5:10 • Revelation 20:11-15

If evil isn't punished, what's the point?
Judgment creates a standard to strive toward

w/out judge, increase of sin

c. In light of these verses, how would you say God's love *works with* His judgment?

His love draws us to obey + judgment keeps you there

But from everlasting to everlasting the Lord's love is with those who fear him, and his righteousness with their children's children—with those who keep his covenant and remember to obey his precepts.

—Psalm 103:17-18 NIV

Delayed Judgment | 95

[G] [7] Psalm 19:9 (NKJV) powerfully declares: "The fear of the Lord is clean, enduring forever." Many have been connected with God through the years. Some have even done mighty acts in His name. But not everyone has endured to the end because not everyone has maintained a healthy fear of the Lord.

a. How do you think the fear of the Lord helps you *endure*? How does it help you stay *clean*?

endure - you realize God is in Control & He'll help you thru it

clean - it makes you not want to sin & displease God, grieve the HS

b. Lucifer once served in the presence of God as a beautiful, anointed cherub—but he didn't endure because of iniquity in his heart. What can you learn from his example?

repent of our sins

guard your heart; keep short accts w/ God

Check out Lucifer's fall in Isaiah 14:12-17; Ezekiel 28:11-18.

c. Read Jesus' words of caution to the disciples in Luke 10:17-20. What is He warning them, and us, to guard against—the thing that got Lucifer kicked out of heaven?

focusing on the power & not the Lord who gives the power

> "Hear me, people of God: You can have the holy anointing oil on you, as Nadab and Abihu did. You can operate in miracles, cast out demons, and heal the sick in His mighty name. You can bring in large offerings to the church like Ananias and Sapphira. You can be anointed for praise and worship like Lucifer. But if you don't possess the fear of the Lord, you are not promised to endure forever. It is the fear of the Lord that causes you to stand before the presence of the Lord forever!"
>
> JOHN BEVERE

8. Have you ever seen the wicked rewarded or hailed as heroes? It can be very frustrating, discouraging, and even enraging. David experienced this too, but God encouraged him by showing Him their end. Read Psalm 37 and answer these questions.

   a. What rewards await the wicked? What is repeatedly declared throughout the scripture?

   Nothing - no rewards

   What they have will be gone + no one will remember them

   b. What promises does God make to the righteous that really encourage you? What is your part in the process of receiving them?

   good things - inherit the land - protection for them + children

   Stay faithful, fear God, obey

   c. God does not want you to be angry, envious, or fretful over evil men. What does He want you to do instead?

   Don't be concerned about evil men but fear the Lord

Check out verses 1-8; 27, 34.

Don't envy sinners, but always continue to fear the Lord. You will be rewarded for this; your hope will not be disappointed.

—Proverbs 23:17-18 NLT

3. Stay close to God; in the Word & prayer

DELAYED JUDGMENT | 97

9 From all that you have learned in the first five sessions, what kinds of things would you say cause a person to *gain* a healthy fear of the Lord? What causes him to *lose* it? What precautionary measures do you feel the Holy Spirit is prompting you to take at this time?

1. a right view of God; a right interpretation of Scripture; a hunger for God; seeking people who have it

2. world's influence; influence of unbelievers; too busy for God

> For we know Him who said, "Vengeance is Mine, I will repay," says the Lord. And again, "The Lord will judge His people." It is a fearful thing to fall into the hands of the living God.
>
> —Hebrews 10:30-31 NKJV
> [emphasis added]

Declaring HIS GREATNESS

"When God's judgments are in the earth, they affect the fear of His name in the hearts of His own people. 'My flesh trembleth for fear of Thee,' said David, 'and I am afraid of Thy judgments' (Psalm 119:120). ...Indeed, many do not regard the works of the Lord, nor take notice of the operation of His hands; and such cannot fear the Lord. But others observe and regard and wisely consider His doings, and the judgments that He executes; and that makes them fear the Lord."

—John Bunyan[3]

3. Stay close to God; praise Him; constant in prayer

 The Blessings of Fearing God

Let those now who reverently and worshipfully fear the Lord say that His mercy and loving-kindness endure forever.

—Psalm 118:4 AMP

The Lord takes pleasure in those who fear Him, in those who hope in His mercy.

—Psalm 147:11 NKJV

For as the heavens are high above the earth, so great is His mercy toward those who fear Him; as far as the east is from the west, so far has He removed our transgressions from us. As a father pities his children, so the Lord pities {*has compassion on*} those who fear Him.

—Psalm 103:11-13 NKJV
[emphasis added]

> **Weekly Activity 5**
>
> ## *Right Where You Live*
> ## ARE YOU SICK AND DON'T KNOW IT?

> *The fear of man will prove to be a snare, but whoever trusts in the Lord is kept safe.*
>
> <u>The fear of human opinion disables</u>; trusting in *God protects you from that.*
>
> —Proverbs 29:25 The Message
> [emphasis added]

You're patiently waiting. Finally, the doctor walks in. After the customary exchange of greetings, he opens his mouth and utters five significant words—words that act as a Geiger counter, leading him to strike upon the most accurate diagnosis of what's going on inside of you. "Tell me how you feel."

Just as we can become physically sick, we can also become spiritually sick. And, one of the most paralyzing sicknesses is *the fear of man*. Now, you may think, *Oh, that's not me; I'm not afraid of people*. However, the fear of man wears many masks. Satan, the enemy of our soul, loves to keep it under wraps. The truth is, most of us catch this disease at some point in life. Therefore, it is good to recognize its symptoms and the remedy. Take a moment to check out this chart.

The Fear of Man
SYNONYMS & SYMPTOMS

Approval Addict
hooked on the approval of others

People Pleaser
driven by desire to please others

Attention Getter
thrives on the attention of others

Appearance Paranoia
obsessed with the way you look and the way you appear to others

Admiration Magnet
addicted to the praise and applause of others

How much does the fear of man influence your life?

Take a moment to *honestly* answer these questions, ranking each item on a scale from one to ten. [Ten being extremely important; one being not important at all. Apply these to your relationships at home, work, church, etc.]

	R	N
Being noticed/acknowledged by others (especially "important" people).	5	9
Being a part of the "in crowd," the center of attention, making people laugh.	1	6
Owning the newest, hottest clothes, car, games, electronic gadgets, etc.	2	3
Receiving compliments on how you look (size, weight, hair, build, clothes, etc.).	3	7
Receiving compliments for the work you do.	6	9
Having your gifts and talents validated and praised by others (friends and leaders).	5	9
Needing others to join in the same activity, ministry, hobby, etc., before you commit.	3	4
Needing others to approve and/or understand your standards, beliefs, and position.	6	8
Telling other people what they want to hear.	7	2
Avoiding the disapproval of others at all costs (for any reason).	4	5
Total Score	42	62

If you scored...

10 to 33 = little to no fear of man • 34 to 66 = mild to moderate fear of man • 67 to 100 = moderate to severe fear of man

Get quiet before the Lord and ask Him to show you the root reasons motivating your actions. Write what He reveals and surrender it all to Him in prayer.

N — I want to matter, be acknowledged for who I am, valued. I didn't feel that as a kid growing up. I didn't feel valued or worthy as an individual by my parents. Or as an adult, especially by my dad.

R Past failures as an adult, criticisms. It's made me afraid to take chances, discouraged me. It put me in a box, made me withdraw from life.

Weekly Devotional 5: FINDING FREEDOM FROM THE FEAR OF MAN

> *The Lord of hosts—regard Him as holy and honor His holy name [by regarding Him as your only hope of safety], and **let Him be your fear and let Him be your dread** [lest you offend Him by your fear of man and distrust of Him]. And He shall be a sanctuary [a sacred and indestructible asylum to those who reverently fear and trust in Him].*
>
> —Isaiah 8:13-14 AMP
> [emphasis added]

Attention, praise, approval, and admiration—it has been the coveted commodity of many men and women since the dawn of creation. Pop culture and modern-day marketing thrive on the energy created by the craze for appearance and what others think. The Bible calls this the *fear of man*, and if we are not careful, the results of its presence in our lives can be deadly. Just look at Ananias and Sapphira, two believers in the early church; they were motivated by the fleshly desire to be noticed—to receive the attention and praise of men. Because their fear of man was greater than their fear of God, they lied to the Holy Spirit and suffered severe, swift judgment.

> "If you desire the praise of man, you will fear man. If you fear man, you will serve man—for you will serve what you fear."
>
> JOHN BEVERE

Jesus was *not a people pleaser*—He had no fear of man and did not seek man's approval. John 2:23-24 says, "While he was in Jerusalem at the Passover Feast, many people saw the miraculous signs he was doing and believed in his name. But Jesus *would not entrust himself to them*, for he knew all men" (NIV, emphasis added). What does it mean that Jesus would not entrust Himself to them? The Contemporary English Version sheds some light on this saying, "Jesus knew what was in their hearts, and he would not *let them have power over him*" (emphasis added). Instead of entrusting Himself to men, who were fickle, He entrusted Himself to God (see 1 Peter 2:23).

Again, in John 6:14-15 we see that "when the people saw him do this miraculous sign, they exclaimed, 'Surely, he is the Prophet we have been expecting!' When Jesus saw that they were ready to force him to be their king, he slipped away into the hills by himself" (NLT). Think about it... The very thing many men fight to have—prestige, position, and power—was Jesus' for the taking, but He walked away from it. Where did He go? Up into the hills—probably to be in the presence of His Father. God was the only one Jesus sought approval and praise from.

> *Do your best to win God's approval as a worker who doesn't need to be ashamed and who teaches only the true message.*
>
> —2 Timothy 2:15 CEV

If you fear men more than God—seeking their approval, praise, and applause—who are you striving to promote? Consequently, who becomes the center of attention enthroned in your life?

Me

How does this contrast with what Jesus says in Matthew 16:24-26?

Jesus says to deny myself

Related scriptures: Mark 8:34-38; Luke 9:23-26.

Ironically, a number of Jewish leaders believed Jesus was the Messiah, but they would not publicly confess their faith for fear of being excommunicated from the synagogue. "For they loved the approval of men rather than the approval of God" (John 12:43 NASB). Is there something about your faith in Christ that you are afraid to publically profess? If so, what is it? *Who* or *what* are you afraid of?

Not being able to defend my faith.

Meditate on the Message

Cheerfully pleasing God is the main thing, and that's what we aim to do, regardless of our conditions. Sooner or later we'll all have to face God, regardless of our conditions. We will appear before Christ and take what's coming to us as a result of our actions, either good or bad.

—*2 Corinthians 5:9-10* The Message

> Be sincere in your motives out of respect for your real master. Whatever you do, do it wholeheartedly as though you were working for your real master and not merely for humans. You know that your real master will give you an inheritance as your reward. It is Christ, your real master, whom you are serving.

—*Colossians 3:22-24* GW

Servants, respectfully obey your earthly masters but always with an eye to obeying the real master, Christ. Don't just do what you have to do to get by, but work heartily, as Christ's servants doing what God wants you to do. And work with a smile on your face, always keeping in mind that no matter who happens to be giving the orders, you're really serving God. Good work will get you good pay from the Master, regardless of whether you are slave or free.

—*Ephesians 6:5-8* The Message

In light of these truths, what should be your *main goal* in life? What has it been up to this point?

Pleasing God! Pleasing myself + wanting others to acknowledge + please me too

What should be the *motivating force* behind all your actions? Why?

Pleasing God, Jesus — He is my master

So, how do we live our lives in the wonderful fear of the Lord? The answer is by God's *grace*. James 4:6 says that God "...gives us more and more **grace** (*power of the Holy Spirit, to meet this evil tendency and all others fully*)" (AMP, emphasis added). The moment we are tempted to give in to the fear of man, we can turn to the Lord and ask Him for grace. This is one of the greatest blessings of being intimately connected in relationship with Christ. We can also receive God's grace to develop the mindset and motivation that empowered Christ throughout His time here on earth. Read John 4:34; 5:19, 30; 12:49, and identify this perspective.

To do God's will

True freedom from the fear of man is attainable. How? John Witherspoon, one of the signers of the Declaration of Independence and president of Princeton College, said it best: "It is only the fear of God that can deliver us from the fear of man."[6] Open your heart wide to the Spirit of the fear of the Lord, and let Him have full reign in your life!

Prayer welcoming the Spirit

> Father, thank you for Your mercy and delaying judgment in my life until my eyes were opened to the truth of the fear of the Lord. Just as Jesus was full of Your Spirit, I desire to be full of Your Spirit. May the Spirit of the Lord rest on me—the Spirit of wisdom and of understanding, the Spirit of counsel and of power, the Spirit of knowledge and of the fear of the Lord—and may I delight in the fear of the Lord (see Isaiah 11:2-3)...in Jesus' name, amen.

☆☆

My Journal
THINGS I WANT TO REMEMBER

> "When irreverence is judged, everyone takes stock of their lives and wrong motives are purged by the light of judgment. This is an atmosphere for true hearts of repentance filled with the fear of God."
>
> JOHN BEVERE

What is the Lord speaking to you through this sobering chapter? What scriptures and principles really hit home? Are there any specific adjustments you feel like He is asking you to make in your life? Take a few moments to hear God's heart and write what you are sensing Him speak.

R- don't be afraid of men re what they think

Quit looking to man for validation. Look to He & My Word for guidance.

CHAPTER OVERVIEW

Society is sick with sin, and to a great degree this includes the church. God's standard of holiness has not changed, so why has His judgment been delayed? It is because His glory is so faint. But, judgment delayed is not judgment denied. Therefore, we must examine ourselves in the light of God's Word and the presence of His Spirit, allowing Him to search our hearts and purify our motives. As we learn to *love God* passionately and *fear Him* reverently, we will grow healthy spiritually. The fear of God will set us free from the fear of man, enabling us to please Him.

(1) Charles R. Swindoll, *The Quest for Character* (Portland, OR: Multnomah Press, 1987) pp. 41-42. (2) Charles Finney, *Spiritual Power, A 30-Day Devotional Treasury* (Lynwood, WA: Emerald Books, 2002) pp. 53-54. (3) Adapted from *Noah Webster's First Edition of an American Dictionary of the English Language* (1828), Republished in facsimile edition by Foundation for American Christian Education (San Francisco, CA, 2000). (4) Robert Morris, *The Blessed Life* (Ventura, CA: Regal Books, 2002) pp. 29-30. (5) John Bunyan, *The Fear of God* (Orlando, FL: Soli Deo Gloria Publications, 2006) p. 79. (6) Quotes by *John Witherspoon* (http://dailychristianquote.com/quoteswa-wl.html#John%20Witherspoon, retrieved 9-15-10).

My Notes

"The glory of this latter temple shall be greater
than the former," says the Lord of hosts.

—Haggai 2:9 NKJV

THE COMING GLORY

Please refer to session 6 of the teaching series, along with chapters 9 and 10 in *The Fear of the Lord* book.

> "I believe with all my heart that we are living in the final days of the church age. The Lord is soon coming back. Prophetic scriptures foretold how God would reveal His glory in a mighty way at the *onset* of the church age and again at the *close* of the church age just prior to His second coming. The early rain began at the day of Pentecost. The latter rain is yet to come!"
>
> JOHN BEVERE

G 1 Many agree that the manifested glory of God in and through the church today is not what it was in the early church in the book of Acts. From our present viewpoint, the former seems more glorious than the latter. But, that is about to change!

    a.   Name some of the amazing manifestations of God's glory in the early church.

_____

_____

_____

For help, **check out** these passages in the book of Acts: 2:1-4, 41; 3:1-10; 12:6-11; 16:25-34; 19:11-12.

b. According to Scripture, the latter rain of God's glory on His church will be *greater* than the former. In light of this, what do you envision this latter rain to look like?

The Significance of Rain

Toward the end of October, heavy rains begin to fall, at intervals, for a day or several days at a time. These are what the Bible calls the **early** or **former rain**. It begins the agricultural year. The soil, which has been hardened and cracked by the long summer, becomes loosened, and the farmer begins plowing and then planting. Till the end of November, the average rainfall is not large, but it increases through December, January, and February. Although the rains do begin to decrease in March and are practically over by the middle of April, the **latter rains** of Scripture are the heavy showers of March and April. Due to their coming *just before the harvest* and the long summer drought, they are far more important to the country than all the rains of the winter months, and that is why these are passed over in Scripture and emphasis is placed on the early and latter rains.[1] To the prophets, rain signified God's continued blessing and favor on His children (see Joel 2:23). Hosea compared God's presence to the refreshing early and latter rains (see Hosea 6:3). A lack of rain was a sign of God's displeasure. God made His gift of rain depend on His people's continued faithfulness (see Deuteronomy 11:13-14).[2]

---

2. After Israel's 70 years in Babylonian captivity, they were allowed to return to their homeland and rebuild. With great zeal, they began rebuilding the temple in Jerusalem. But within a few years, the project came to a standstill. Sixteen years passed, and the temple was still not completed.

   a. According to Haggai 1:1-11, what caused the delay and their passionate zeal to fade? How did God respond to this? (See verses 9-11.)

   Attention to their own homes + needs. God w/held rain; their efforts were unfulfilled

b. How do you think this example relates to what is going on with the church today?

We're more busy w/ our own needs than God's. We're not prospering.

c. Can you personally identify with this situation? If so, in what ways? What is the Lord prompting you to do to resume work on His *temple*?

Where can I be of use in the Church?

3. Again, during the days of Malachi the prophet, the people of Israel became sidetracked in their devotion to God. This time they began bringing Him animals that were blind, crippled and diseased to offer as sacrifices (see Malachi 1:6-8). Basically, they were keeping the best for themselves and giving God the leftovers. He viewed it as irreverence.

a. Take a moment and examine your life. Is there an area in which you know that you are not giving your best—and instead, giving your leftovers? If so, where? *food (gifts)*

N Being more generous for myself than others.
Using my time for myself over others. (Rick)
Looking to myself in scheduling rather than God.
Wasting my time

Review your roles as a spouse, a parent, a child, an employee/employer, a volunteer, etc.

N away of His word - praying

b. In light of your previous answer, pray and ask the Lord how you can rise to the next level in these areas. Write what He stirs in your heart.

N Be more generous to others
Put others first; their needs first
Ask God re schedule
Limit TV, computer games

R- give more to Christian organizations
- join AMAC, Heritage

> *Oh, that you would burst forth from the skies and come down! How the mountains would quake in your presence! The consuming fire of your glory would burn down the forests and boil the oceans dry. The nations would tremble before you; then your enemies would learn the reason for your fame! So it was before when you came down, for you did awesome things beyond our highest expectations, and how the mountains quaked! For since the world began no one has seen or heard of such a God as ours, who works for those who wait for him!*
>
> —Isaiah 64:1-4 TLB

4 In order to be fully in tune with what God is about to do in the coming days, it is important to keep our priorities straight. Stop and ask yourself, *What things are most important to me—what are my top priorities?*

a. List the top five priorities in your life in order (number one being most important).

N
1) God   R 1) God
2) husband   2) wife
3) family   3) Ed + Gretchen
4) friends   4) secondary family re Suz
5) service/self   5) myself

b. Now, take a look at your *calendar* and *checkbook* over the past few months. Do they confirm your list? If not, ask the Lord what changes you can make to get things in order.

_____
_____
_____
_____
_____

Where we invest our time and money most is a strong indicator of our priorities in life. **Check out** Matthew 6:20-21, 33.

> "We must keep in mind God's purpose for creation. He did not put Adam in the garden to have a worldwide preaching, healing, or deliverance ministry. Adam was placed in the garden so God could walk with Him. We have been created for God—to coexist with His glory. That is His goal for you."
>
> **JOHN BEVERE**

5 Honoring God with first place in your life is an expression of the fear of the Lord. Read these verses and identify the blessings associated with making your relationship with Him top priority.

> But seek (aim at and strive after) first of all His kingdom and His righteousness (His way of doing and being right), and then all these things taken together will be given you besides.
>
> —*Matthew 6:33* AMP

> Yes, I am the vine; you are the branches. Those who remain in me, and I in them, will produce much fruit. For apart from me you can do nothing. But if you remain in me and my words remain in you, you may ask for anything you want, and it will be granted!
>
> —*John 15:5, 7* NLT

> Yet those who wait for the Lord will gain new strength; they will mount up with wings like eagles, they will run and not get tired, they will walk and not become weary.
>
> —*Isaiah 40:31* NASB

> The one thing I ask of the Lord—the thing I seek most—is to live in the house of the Lord all the days of my life, delighting in the Lord's perfections and meditating in his Temple. For he will conceal me there when troubles come; he will hide me in his sanctuary. He will place me out of reach on a high rock.
>
> —*Psalm 27:4-5* NLT

Related scriptures: Psalm 119:2; Proverbs 3:5-8; Mark 12:29-30.

a. The blessings that come from putting God first include…

  *** all else will be given.
  *** anything you want will be granted.
  *** you won't grow tired or weary
  *** you will be out of reach by trouble.

b. How are you challenged and encouraged by these verses?

  WOW

Think About It

"Why do some persons 'find' God in a way that others do not? Why does God manifest His presence to some and let multitudes of others struggle along in the half-light of imperfect Christian experience? Of course, the will of God is the same for all. He has no favorites within His household. All He has ever done for any of His children He will do for all of His children. The difference lies not with God but with us.

Pick at random a score of great saints whose lives and testimonies are widely known. Let them be Bible characters or well-known Christians of post-biblical times. …I venture to suggest that the one vital quality which they had in common was spiritual receptivity. Something in them was open to heaven, something which urged them Godward. Without attempting anything like a profound analysis, I shall say simply that they had spiritual awareness and that they went on to cultivate it until it became the biggest thing in their lives. They differed from the average person in that *when they felt the inward longing they did something about it.* They acquired the lifelong habit of spiritual response. They were not disobedient to the heavenly vision. As David put it neatly, 'When thou saidst, Seek ye my face; my heart said unto thee, Thy face, Lord, will I seek' (Psalm 27:8)."

—A. W. Tozer[3]

[G] 6. David was a man after God's own heart. His passion was to see the glory of God restored to the nation of Israel. That is why he wanted to bring the Ark of the Covenant back to Jerusalem. Although his motives were pure and honorable, something was wrong with his method.

a. Who did David consult with before moving the Ark the *first* time? Who apparently influenced the methods he used? What was the result of their efforts?

Check out 1 Chronicles 13:1-14. Also, compare 1 Samuel 6:1-2; 7-8 with 2 Samuel 6:1-4.

b. How does this example compare with the things we are doing for God today? What does it say to you?

c. Before David tried to move the Ark the *second* time, what did he do? Who or what did he consult? What does this say to you personally?

Ask God before acting

Check out 1 Chronicles 15:2, 12-13.

G 7 Irreverent attitudes and behavior toward God are major hindrances holding back the "latter rain" of His glory. By giving God reverence and honor, you can help usher in a fresh manifestation of His glory in the church today. Pray and ask the Lord to show you how you can bring God glory at church, at home, in your giving, through serving others, etc.

Ways I can show God reverence and honor include…

N 1) *putting Rick first. Showing him respect + love by more words + actions when no one but God is looking*

2) *Wherever I go, go w/ attitude of service to others, obedience to God, not my agenda.*

R 1) *raising my hands when we sing*
2) *get on knees when I pray*
3) *pray more consistently w/ wife*

> **Declaring**
> **HIS GREATNESS**
>
> "A holy life will produce the deepest impression. Lighthouses blow no horns; they only shine."
> —D.L. Moody[4]

8. All through the book of Acts, we see the disciples of Jesus performing signs and wonders wherever they went. After these miracles took place, many people repented and put their faith in the Lord. This harvest of souls is the precious fruit of the earth produced by the early rain of God's glory. There is another harvest yet to come.

   a. How important is it to you to see souls birthed into God's family? How important is it to God? — *very*

   Check out 1 Timothy 2:1-4; 2 Peter 3:9.

   b. Who among your family and friends are you believing will come to the Lord before He returns?

   Continue to lift up your loved ones. Your fervent, heartfelt prayers are making a difference (see James 5:16).

   c. *Get quiet before the Lord.* Ask Him, "What needs to change in me so that Your miracles can manifest through me and Your church?" Surrender these things to Him in prayer.

   R — I need to fear God more than people

   N — I need to put God & His work first — all else is secondary
   — I need to reach out to people — ask God who I need to contact, help, encourage — seek God's direction

The fruit of the righteous is a tree of life, and he who wins souls is wise.

—Proverbs 11:30 NKJV

> "The latter rain always brought in the greater harvest. The greatest harvest of souls the world has ever seen come into the kingdom is going to happen in this last generation. I want to believe with all my heart that we are a part of that generation."
>
> **JOHN BEVERE**

G 9. In preparation of God's coming glory, He wants us to enlarge our vision and expand our expectations of what He can do in and through us. This coming glory will be seven times greater than the former.

a. Read Isaiah 30:18 AMP (emphasis added), and write what the Holy Spirit reveals to you about the rewards of expecting great things from God.

And therefore the Lord [earnestly] waits [expecting, looking, and longing] to be gracious to you; and therefore He lifts Himself up, that He may have mercy on you and show loving-kindness to you. For the Lord is a God of justice. Blessed (happy, fortunate, to be envied) are all those who [earnestly] wait for Him, who *expect* and *look* and *long for Him* [for His victory, His favor, His love, His peace, His joy, and His matchless, unbroken companionship]!

graciousness, mercy, loving-kindness, blessing

Declaring
HIS GREATNESS

"...Expectation is the breeding ground of the miraculous. Dare to stick it out; dare to take your place in this magnificent moment in history. For who knows what is just around the corner? I sense that the water is rising, the spiritual tide is rising, and we are about to experience a mighty crash, like a tidal wave, as our desire to serve Him consumes us. If you want it, it's already there. We are on the brink of something miraculous, so I'm encouraging everyone in the church to get ready."

—Darlene Zschech[3]

b. What vision has God placed in your heart? What are you longing for Him to bring about in your life, the lives of your loved ones, and the lives of those around you?

R- see a revival in the World

> *God can do anything, you know—far more than you could ever imagine or guess or request in your wildest dreams! He does it not by pushing us around but by working within us, his Spirit deeply and gently within us. Glory to God in the church! Glory to God in the Messiah, in Jesus! Glory down all the generations! Glory through all millennia! Oh, yes!*
>
> —Ephesians 3:20-21 The Message

> "Where we've been and where we are now is not where we are headed. We must raise our eyes to the horizon and look for His coming glory. There will be a major difference between today's church and the early church. The glory of the latter will be greater than the former."
>
> JOHN BEVERE

The Blessings of Fearing God

Then the church throughout Judea, Galilee and Samaria enjoyed a time of peace. It was strengthened; and encouraged by the Holy Spirit, it grew in numbers, living in the fear of the Lord.

—Acts 9:31 NIV

Praise the Lord! How joyful are those who fear the Lord and delight in obeying his commands. Their children will be successful everywhere; an entire generation of godly people will be blessed. They themselves will be wealthy, and their good deeds will last forever.

—Psalm 112:1-3 NLT

While Jesus was here on earth, he offered prayers and pleadings, with a loud cry and tears, to the one who could rescue him from death. And God heard his prayers because of his deep reverence for God.

—Hebrews 5:7 NLT

> **Weekly Activity 6**
>
> *Right Where You Live*
> ## EXPERIENCING THE WORD OF HIS POWER

Is there an area of your life in which you would like to see the glory of God manifesting more? An area where His character mirrored in your life is lacking? Here's great news—it can change! What has always been does not have to always be. God has given you the indestructible, unchangeable Word of His power to destroy even the most stubborn patterns of wrong thinking and behavior.

How powerful is God's Word?
Is not My word like *fire* [that consumes all that cannot endure the test]? says the Lord, and like a *hammer* that breaks in pieces the rock [of most stubborn resistance]?

—*Jeremiah* 23:29 AMP

For the Word that God speaks is *alive* and *full of power* [making it active, operative, energizing, and effective]; it is sharper than any two-edged sword, penetrating to the dividing line of the breath of life (soul) and [the immortal] spirit, and of joints and marrow [of the deepest parts of our nature], exposing and sifting and analyzing and judging the very thoughts and purposes of the heart.

—*Hebrews* 4:12 AMP

In a humble (gentle, modest) spirit receive and welcome the Word which implanted and rooted [in your hearts] contains the power to save your souls.

—*James* 1:21 AMP
[emphasis added]

Related scriptures: Psalm 107:20; Romans 1:16; John 8:31-32.

PUT IT TO THE TEST! APPLY THE WORD TO YOUR LIFE.

- **Choose an area of your life** where you want to see the glory of God manifesting more. For example, maybe you need discipline in the area of your mind to overcome worry and anxiety.

- **Find scriptures in God's Word** declaring your ability in Christ to have God's character instead of the character you currently see. Again, if worry and anxiety are a problem, find verses on God's peace and faithfulness, such as Matthew 6:24-34, 1 Peter 5:7, and Philippians 4:6-8.

- **Read them out loud** a few times a day. Commit to proclaiming God's Word over your life for the next 30 days. Personalize each passage. Say things like, "I do not worry about what I will eat or drink; God cares for the birds of the air, and He will certainly care for me."

- **Observe in amazement** what takes place in your life as a result.

- **Journal your experience** and write down anything the Lord reveals to you.

Pen your progress

Date Started: _____

_____
_____
_____
_____
_____

Date Completed: _____

DIG INTO GOD'S PRICELESS TREASURE!

I rejoice in your word like one who discovers a great treasure.

—Psalm 119:162 NLT

How do you view the Bible? Hopefully you don't see it as just a nice book filled with interesting stories or a long list of "dos and don'ts." It is an everlasting masterpiece unlike any other book on earth. It is the life-giving, inspired Word of God that is truly a priceless treasure. The psalmist said, "Truth from your mouth means more to me than striking it rich in a gold mine" (Psalm 119:72 The Message).

Charles Colson, dynamic leader of Prison Fellowship Ministries and inspiring author and speaker, offers this insightful perspective on the Holy Scriptures:

"The Bible—banned, burned, beloved. More widely read, more frequently attacked than any other book in history. Generations of intellectuals have attempted to discredit it; dictators of every age have outlawed it and executed those who read it. Yet soldiers carry it into battle believing it more powerful than their weapons. Fragments of it smuggled into solitary prison cells have transformed ruthless killers into gentle saints. Pieced-together scraps of Scripture have converted whole villages of pagan Indians. ...Literary classics endure the centuries. Philosophers mold the thoughts of generations unborn. Modern media shapes current culture. Yet nothing has affected the rise and fall of civilization, the character of cultures, the structure of governments, and the lives of the inhabitants of this planet as profoundly as the words of the Bible."

—Charles Colson[6]

Indeed, if there was ever a book that has been under fire, the Bible is it—especially in today's society. But think about it... Why is it attacked so much? There must be something to this collection of 66 books written over the span of 1600 years by 40 different people—something incredibly powerful that threatens the enemies of God and empowers His people.

Meditate on the Message

The main thing to keep in mind here is that no prophecy of Scripture is a matter of private opinion. And why? Because it's not something concocted in the human heart. Prophecy resulted when the Holy Spirit prompted men and women to speak God's Word.

—2 *Peter* 1:20-21 The Message

All Scripture is inspired by God and is useful to teach us what is true and to make us realize what is wrong in our lives. It corrects us when we are wrong and teaches us to do what is right. God uses it to prepare and equip his people to do every good work.

—2 *Timothy* 3:16-17 NLT

• • • • • •

For everything that was written in the past was written to teach us, so that through endurance and the encouragement of the Scriptures we might have hope.

—*Romans* 15:4 NIV

> These things happened to make them an example for others. These things were written down as a warning for us who are living in the closing days of history.
>
> —*1 Corinthians 10:11* GW

According to these verses, who wrote the Word of God?

God

For what reasons was it written?

to teach, warn, help us understand our need of a relat w/ God

Is the Bible an outdated book, or is it relevant to you today? How do you know it can be trusted?
Check out 1 Peter 1:24-25 • Matthew 5:18 • Psalm 12:6; 119:89 • Numbers 23:19

What are some of the treasures that Scripture holds for you as you regularly feed your spirit?
Check out Joshua 1:8 • Psalm 1:1-3; 19:7-11 • 1 Peter 2:2 • Deuteronomy 11:18-21

Currently, how vital is the Word of God to your life? How does your day-to-day lifestyle prove this?

*Your words are what sustain me; they are food to my hungry soul.
They bring joy to my sorrowing heart and delight me.
How proud I am to bear your name, O Lord.*

—Jeremiah 15:16 TLB

> "If the church really pressed in to the fear of the Lord, I believe we would see God's glory restored in the church. I believe if we all became hungry for the Word of God to the point where we applied our heart to wisdom and cried out for understanding and sought it as hidden treasure, we would again see the fear of the Lord in the church."
>
> **JOHN BEVERE**

Why is the Word of God important to you? If you had 30 seconds or less to encourage the world to read and study Scripture, what would you say?

_____
_____
_____

Name your top three "jewels" from Scripture. Why are these verses special to you? How have they transformed your life?

R *I can do all things thru Christ who gives me strength*

N *Taste & see that the Lord is good.*

_____

The wealth of God's Word is waiting to be excavated. An invitation is extended to you to explore its riches, and the Holy Spirit is ready to reveal its priceless truths. Do you want a greater hunger for God's Word and an understanding of its meaning? Pray this prayer from your heart:

Prayer for hunger and learning
Father, thank you for the priceless gift of Your Word. It is truly a treasure. Forgive me for neglecting it in any way. Give me an insatiable hunger to

read and study it. May Your truth not just go in one ear and out the other. May it find a permanent place in my heart and soul. Holy Spirit, be my teacher. Scripture says that You permanently abide in me to lead me and guide me into all truth (see 1 John 2:27; John 14:26; 16:13). Give me ears to hear what You are teaching me; give me total recall of Your truth. May I always put You first in my life and seek You for wisdom and direction in every endeavor. You are awesome, Lord, and I long to see Your coming glory… in Jesus' name, amen!

My Journal
THINGS I WANT TO REMEMBER

God's best is yet to come! The glory that is coming on us, His church, in these last days will outshine every move and manifestation in previous generations. Are you preparing for Him? Are you growing in your understanding and appreciation of the fear of the Lord? Take a few moments to jot down anything you sense the Holy Spirit speaking to your heart.

___

___

___

___

___

> **CHAPTER OVERVIEW**
> God began to pour out His Spirit upon all flesh on the day of Pentecost. That was the "early rain" of His glory. But God is not finished. There is a "latter rain" that is about to burst forth upon His church in the days ahead. Through the fear of the Lord, we can draw close to His heart, receive wisdom and direction in His Word, and be ready for the arrival of His manifested presence. It's time to put God first, expand your expectations, and prepare to be amazed!

---

(1) Adapted from *The New Unger's Bible Dictionary*, Merrill F. Unger (Chicago, IL: Moody Press, Revised and Updated Edition, 1988). (2) *Nelson's Illustrated Encyclopedia of Bible Facts*; James I. Packer, Merrill C. Tenney, William White, Jr. Editors (Nashville, TN: Thomas Nelson Publishers, 1995) p. 184. (3) A.W. Tozer, *The Pursuit of God* (Camp Hill, PA: Christian Publications, Inc., 1993) pp. 62-63. (4) *Fast Break: Five-Minute Devotions to Start Your Day* (St. San Luis Obispo, CA: Parable, 2007) Day 334. (5) Darlene Zschech, *Extravagant Worship* (Bloomington, MN: Bethany House Publishers, 2001, 2002) pp. 154-155. (6) Charles Colson, *Loving God* (Grand Rapids, MI: Judith Markham Books, 1983) p. 55.

My Notes

*Whenever someone turns to the Lord, the veil is taken away.
For the Lord is the Spirit, and wherever
the Spirit of the Lord is, there is freedom.*

*So all of us who have had that veil removed
can see and reflect the glory of the Lord.*

*And the Lord—who is the Spirit—makes us more and more
like him as we are changed into his glorious image.*

—2 Corinthians 3:16-18 NLT

FROM GLORY TO GLORY

Please refer to session 7 of the teaching series, along with chapters 11 and 12 in *The Fear of the Lord* book.

> "As we behold the glory of the Lord in the *mirror* of His revealed Word, we are 'being transformed [changed] into the same image of the Lord from glory to glory.' This describes the process the Bible calls 'working out' our salvation."
>
> JOHN BEVERE

1. In the New Covenant, God's plan is not for us to *reflect* His glory, but for His glory *to emanate from us!* (See 2 Corinthians 3:10.) Sadly, the Israelites missed the glory of the Old Covenant because their minds were blinded to what they needed so desperately to see. Paul warns us so that we might not find ourselves blind and in the same dilemma.[1]

    a. What caused their minds to be blinded?

    Their hearts were not inclined to fear God or keep His commandments

    Check out Deuteronomy 5:28-29.

    b. The Israelites relied on Moses to hear from God for them because they were afraid of His presence. Have you, in any way, been relying on your pastor or a preacher to hear from God for you, meanwhile withdrawing from His presence? If so, why?

Get quiet before the Lord. Repent and ask Him to reveal your true heart's condition and how *He* sees you. Take time to simply enjoy being in His presence. He is longing for you to draw near!

[G] 2. If there is anything we need God's grace to help us stay away from, it is murmuring and complaining. Murmuring and complaining are *transformation stoppers*. They show a lack of the fear of the Lord, which in this case is a lack of faith in who God is and what He says. The Scripture inseparably links this attitude with rebellion and unbelief.

a. Read Numbers 14:20-35 and Hebrews 3:12-4:1. What happened to the Israelites as a result of their complaining and unbelief?

They died in the desert & never got to enter the land. They were killed by the destroying angel.

Related scripture: 1 Corinthians 10:10.

b. What does this example say to you, and how does it motivate you?

God doesn't like complaining & grumbling. It shows Him contempt. He will not let it pass.
I don't want to complain against what God has given me or placed me, but be thankful.

c. Instead of murmuring, complaining, or having a meltdown when an issue arises, what does God want you to do?

Trust in Him; pray & petition Him; cast all your anxieties on Him; lean on God not self & He will make paths straight.

Check out Philippians 4:6-7; 1 Peter 5:6-7; Proverbs 3:5-6.

d. Is there any area or situation in your life that you've recently had the wrong attitude toward? If so, what is it? How can you begin to see it from God's perspective?

Rain - better than fires or tornados, no floods, no water rationing - enjoy the respites

> *Do all things without grumbling and faultfinding and complaining [against God] and questioning and doubting [among yourselves].*
>
> —Philippians 2:14 AMP

> "Complaining is a symptom of a lack of the fear of the Lord and the first sign that we are *drifting toward disobedience*. God hates it. It is one of the five sins that kept Israel from the Promised Land. Why does God hate complaining? Because complaining says to God, 'I don't like what You're doing in my life, and if I were You, I'd do it differently.'"
>
> **JOHN BEVERE**

3. Instead of complaining, God wants us to be *thankful*. Thankfulness is an expression of the fear of the Lord, and it opens the gate to His presence (see Psalm 100:4). By His grace, we can learn to cultivate an attitude of gratitude and experience His transforming power at work in us.

a. When others are thankful to you, how does it make you feel? What does it make you want to do? How do you think your thankfulness makes God feel?

It makes me feel good, appreciated, that what I did was beneficial to someone else. It makes me want to do more. It would be the same for God.

b. What tends to cause you to complain or be ungrateful? How can you overcome/avoid these things?

Nan - things don't go my way or don't work or no communicated - makes me frustrated + complain. Put God in the picture.

Rick - surprises or changes in sched that I'm not planning on. Learn to be more flexible.

c. What helps you have a grateful, thankful heart and mouth? How can you encourage these things?

Nan - when good or unexpected good things happen. Look for good.

Rick - seeing others worse off than me. Listen to Joni.

> *Always be joyful. Never stop praying. **Be thankful** in all circumstances, for this is God's will for you who belong to Christ Jesus.*
>
> —1 Thessalonians 5:16-18 NLT
> [emphasis added]

Declaring His Greatness

"Where your pleasure is, there is your treasure; where your treasure is, there is your heart; where your heart is, there is your happiness."
—Augustine

4 A thankful heart is a happy heart—a happiness that is not based on circumstances but on the unchanging truth of who God is and who we are in Him. This is the *peace* Jesus gives us in John 14:27. This is the *joy of the Lord* that is our strength talked about in Nehemiah 8:10. This is true *contentment*!

Meditate on the Message

Yet true godliness with contentment is itself great wealth. After all, we brought nothing with us when we came into the world, and we can't take anything with us when we leave it. So if we have enough food and clothing, let us be content.

—1 Timothy 6:6-8 NLT

Keep your lives free from the love of money and be content with what you have, because God has said, "Never will I leave you; never will I forsake you." So we say with confidence, "The Lord is my helper; I will not be afraid. What can man do to me?"

—*Hebrews 13:5-6* NIV

I've *learned* by now to be quite content whatever my circumstances. I'm just as happy with little as with much, with much as with little. I've found the recipe for being happy whether full or hungry, hands full or hands empty. Whatever I have, wherever I am, I can make it through anything in the One who makes me who I am.

—*Philippians 4:11-13* The Message
[emphasis added]

a. In light of these verses, what would you say is the "recipe" for true contentment?

Rick – if you have enuf clothes or food – you are content

Nan – trust in God

b. What do you think is the connection between thankfulness, contentment, and seeing God's glorious character created in you?

Rick –

Nan – When we're thankful & content, we're showing our trust in God for us. That trust allows God to shine through us.

> "Only those with unveiled hearts can behold Him. Obedience to God keeps your eyes uncovered and your heart unveiled. As we behold His glory in the mirror of His revealed Word, we are changed into His image by the Spirit of God! We are changed into what we behold."
>
> JOHN BEVERE

G 5 *Obedience* is the key ingredient needed to see God's glory produced in your life. In short, obedience is to yield your will to His—to fully do what He asks you to do. Obeying God not only shows your faith in Him; it is also a true expression of the fear of the Lord.

Read 2 Corinthians 3:16-18, James 1:22-25, and Ephesians 4:17-24.

a. How does *dis*obedience to God place a "veil" over your heart? What is this veil?

Nan - veil = sin; constricts God's influence

b. How does obedience keep the veil removed from your heart and allow you to grow in His glory?

Rick - if you're obedient you don't sin

Nan - no constraints

c. *Get quiet before the Lord.* Ask Him to search your heart and reveal any area of partial obedience or disobedience. Write what He reveals and surrender it to Him in prayer.

Once you repent, receive His forgiveness; and, if the opportunity to fully obey is still available, carry out His request.

6. Read Isaiah 66:2 and Jeremiah 5:22. To "tremble at His Word" is to willingly obey God even when you don't understand and it appears more advantageous to compromise or not obey His Word.[3]

a. Has this definition proven true in your life? If so, what was the situation and what did you choose to do? What was the outcome?

G **7** All through Scripture, God connects trials, troubles, pruning, and suffering synonymously with His chastening or discipline. The truth is, none of these things sound appealing. Yet, they are actually positive things that produce God's glory in our lives.

> ### Declaring HIS GREATNESS
>
> "God's revelations are sealed to us until they are opened to us by *obedience*. You will never get them open by philosophy or thinking. Immediately you obey, a flash of light comes. Let God's truth work in you by soaking in it, not by worrying into it. *Obey God* in the thing He is at present showing you, and instantly the next thing is opened up. ...God will never reveal more truth about Himself till you obey what you know already."
> —*Oswald Chambers*[4]

a. Read Hebrews 12:5-11, and in your own words, explain how God's discipline works to produce His glory in your life.

Nan - its for our good to share in God's holiness. It produces righteousness + peace

Related scriptures: John 15:1-2, Deuteronomy 8:2-6; Proverbs 15:5.

b. What *good* things happen in you and for you as a result of receiving discipline or going through trials?

Rick - I feel sense of accomplishment thru trials

Nan - learning, stretching, understanding = becoming more mature

Check out 2 Corinthians 4:17; James 1:2-4, 12; 5:11; 1 Peter 1:6-7; 4:12-16.

c. The hardships we face reveal the true content of our hearts—what we truly believe. Take a few moments to recall past situations and experiences, what you learned about yourself and God, and how you grew as a result.

d. If you're a Christian and you seldom experience trials or opposition, what might this indicate?

_____
_____
_____

Consider Revelation 3:15-16.

DISCIPLINE AND SELF-CONTROL

Discipline means "to train or develop by **instruction** and **exercise** especially in self-control."[5] *Self-control,* or *temperance,* is "moderation, particularly in regard to the indulgence of the natural, fleshly appetites and passions."[6] To be a *disciplined* believer means to be continually *instructed* and *trained* by God's Word, God's Spirit, and God-ordained difficulties. When we choose to receive God's grace and obey His instruction, especially in the midst of difficulties, His Spirit develops the fruit of self-control in us. As a result, godly habits are formed in place of ungodly ones. If you are receiving discipline, you can know that you are a true son or daughter of God.

> "We have two choices as believers: We can relinquish complete ownership of our lives to Jesus, or we can retain it and remain trapped under the dominion of deception. If we fear God, we will yield completely to His authority and His kingship. This allows Him full and unrestricted possession of us. We literally become His bondservants."
>
> JOHN BEVERE

[G] 8 Jesus said, "The Son of Man came *not* to be served but **to serve** others and to give his life as a ransom for many" (Mark 10:45 NLT, emphasis added). Next to fellowshipping with the Father, being a Christian is about serving Christ and others. When we surrender ownership of our lives to the Lord in reverential fear, there are countless blessings that come to us.

a. In your own words, explain what it means to call Jesus Christ "Lord."

R&N – He is in control of my life

b. *Get quiet before the Lord.* Evaluate your life—your priorities, day-to-day tasks and activities, choices, etc. What areas, if any, are you still "owning"? What practical ways can you "lose your life" and serve the Lord and those in your life in a greater capacity?

R – ask Him what to do

N – pray over sched, daily quiet time, everything

c. What blessings did Jesus say would be given to you for surrendering your life to Him? Read Matthew 19:27-30 for the answer.

– be given 100 times as much
– eternal life

Related scripture: Mark 10:28-31.

> "What happens when we are submitted to the Lord Jesus, trembling at His Word? Paul tells us in 2 Corinthians 3:16, 'Whenever a person turns [in repentance] to the Lord, the veil is stripped off and taken away' (AMP). When you turn to the lordship of Jesus, which is synonymous with fearing God, the veil is taken away!"
>
> **JOHN BEVERE**

9. Second Corinthians 3:18 declares that we are changed *progressively* into God's image from one degree of glory to another. This is what it means to work out our salvation. The three indispensable ingredients that fuel this transformation are God's Word, God's Holy Spirit, and having a willing, obedient heart.

Meditate on the Message

But he who looks carefully into the faultless law, the [law] of liberty, and is faithful to it and perseveres in looking into it, being not a heedless listener who forgets but an active doer [who obeys], he shall be blessed in his doing (his life of obedience).

—*James 1:25* AMP

For God, who said, "Let there be light in the darkness," has made this light shine in our hearts so we could know the glory of God that is seen in the face of Jesus Christ. We now have this light shining in our hearts, but we ourselves are like fragile clay jars containing this great treasure. This makes it clear that our great power is from God, not from ourselves.

—*2 Corinthians 4:6-7* NLT

We couldn't be more sure of what we saw and heard—God's glory, God's voice. The prophetic Word was confirmed to us. You'll do well to keep focusing on it. It's the one light you have in a dark time as you wait for daybreak and the rising of the Morning Star in your hearts.

—*2 Peter 1:19* The Message

a. What is the Lord showing you in these verses? Can you see your part in the process of transformation?

   Allow God to work in us + be obedient

b. What common threads can you identify that relate to experiencing God's glory?

   obedience
   intention in seeking God

10. What is the ever-increasing outcome of our glorious transformation? Consider these promises and write what the Lord reveals to you.

The way of the righteous is like the first gleam of dawn, which shines ever brighter until the full light of day.

—*Proverbs 4:18* NLT

The light of the [uncompromisingly] righteous [is within him—it grows brighter and] rejoices, but the lamp of the wicked [furnishes only a derived, temporary light and] shall be put out shortly.

—Proverbs 13:9 AMP

Arise, shine; for your light has come, and the glory of the Lord has risen upon you. For behold, darkness will cover the earth and deep darkness the peoples; but the Lord will rise upon you and His glory will appear upon you. Nations will come to your light, and kings to the brightness of your rising.

—Isaiah 60:1-3 NASB

Declaring His Greatness

"He is intangible and invisible. But His work is more powerful than the most ferocious wind. The Spirit brings order out of chaos and beauty out of ugliness. He can transform a sin-blistered man into a paragon of virtue. The Spirit changes people. The Author of life is also the Transformer of life."

—R. C. Sproul

Related scriptures: Matthew 13:43; Daniel 12:3; Isaiah 58:10.

You'll be like Jesus

You will get better + better, more reflection of God within you

The Blessings of Fearing God

And this is what he says to all humanity: "The fear of the Lord is true wisdom; to forsake evil is real understanding."

—Job 28:28 NLT

The reverent and worshipful fear of the Lord is the beginning and the principal and choice part of knowledge [its starting point and its essence]; but fools despise skillful and godly Wisdom, instruction, and discipline.

—Proverbs 1:7 AMP

The fear of the Lord is the beginning of wisdom, and the knowledge of the Holy One is understanding.

—Proverbs 9:10 NKJV

The fear of the Lord teaches a man wisdom, and humility comes before honor.

—Proverbs 15:33 NIV

Weekly Activity 7

Right Where You Live
TRACKING YOUR TRANSFORMATION

Remember when you were a kid you were often anxious to see how much you had grown? You would walk up to your father, mother, or an older sibling and measure yourself against them with your hand to see how tall you were. Maybe you even had lines drawn on the edge of a door or on the wall, showing your height and age as you grew through the years. It was so exciting to see those lines move three, four, or five inches! It was a sign you were growing.

Well, if you have been feeding yourself the life-changing truth of God's Word, obeying what the Holy Spirit reveals, fellowshipping with the Father and committed believers, **you have been growing** spiritually. True, it is not always easy to see growth in our own lives, but here are a few ways to measure what God has been doing in you.

Reflect on your past

Sit quietly and take a careful, prayerful look at your life over the past few years. What things did you do *then* that you no longer do *now*? For instance, did you struggle with fear, lying, controlling your anger, etc., but by God's grace you have overcome it? These are all areas of growth—positive proof of God's transforming power at work in you! *Get quiet before the Lord.* Ask Him to show you how you have grown and what actions He had you take to see victory in your life.

Wrong behaviors/habits	Action(s) God prompted me to take to see victory
I used to	
I used to	
I used to	
I used to	
I used to	
I used to	
I used to	

Get feedback from friends

Another great way to track your transformation is to sit with a few trusted friends and ask them how you've grown. These should be seasoned believers who care about you and have watched your life for a number of years. Ask them candidly,

"How have I changed over the years? Where can you see growth in my life? What attitudes/actions did I have/do that I no longer have/do?" Write down what they say. Again, ask the Holy Spirit to remind you how you overcame.

Looking forward to future growth
After looking over all your findings, what can you learn from the past and apply to future growth? Do you see any patterns? What common denominators consistently helped bring growth and transformation?

_____

_____

_____

Remember, the greatest agent of transformation is God's Word (review Chapter 6, *Experiencing the Word of His Power* and *Dig into God's Priceless Treasure*). There is life-transforming power in you speaking God's Word aloud over your life!

THERE'S POWER IN YOUR WORDS!

> *Words satisfy the mind as much as fruit does the stomach; good talk is as gratifying as a good harvest. Death and life are in the power of the tongue, and they who indulge in it shall eat the fruit of it [for death or life].*
>
> —Proverbs 18:20-21
> Verse 20 The Message; verse 21 AMP

Words. What power they have! How important the arrangement of those 26 letters of the English alphabet that roll off our tongues! Words can strengthen, encourage, and instill life, or they can bring great destruction. God has given us tremendous creative power, and it is right under our noses. By learning to harness the power of our words, we can see great things happen in our lives and the lives of others.

As we learned earlier, murmuring and complaining are transformation stoppers. They are negative words producing death. Thanksgiving and praise, on the other hand, are forms of life. They bring us into the presence of the Lord and help produce the positive transformation into His image that we long for. **Joyce Meyer**, a powerful minister of the Word who has spoken extensively on this topic, said...

"We can bless ourselves or curse ourselves by the way we speak. When we bless, we speak well of; when we curse, we speak evil of. You and I can bless our own lives and bring joy to them, or we can curse them and bring misery upon ourselves, by the words of our mouth."[8]

God confirms the power of the tongue through James. He explains, "We put bits in the mouths of horses to make them obey us, and we have control over everything they do. The same thing is true for ships. They are very big and are driven by strong winds. Yet, by using small rudders, pilots steer ships wherever they want them to go. In the same way the *tongue* is a small part of the body, but it can brag about doing important things." (James 3:3-5 GW, emphasis added). James goes on to say in verses 7 and 8 that "people have tamed all kinds of animals, birds, reptiles, and sea creatures. Yet, no one can tame the tongue. It is an uncontrollable evil filled with deadly poison."

At this point, you may be thinking, *Well, if no man can tame the tongue, how can we bring it under control?* The answer is by the help of God. Indeed, "...with man this is impossible, but with God **all** things are possible" (Matthew 19:26 NIV, emphasis added).

Read Proverbs 13:3; 21:23, and Psalm 39:1; 141:3. What do these verses say to you, and how are you challenged by them?

It's imp to guard carefully what I say. Lord, help me control what I say

According to Psalm 35:28, 49:3, 51:15, and 71:15, what kinds of things should we speak with our mouths?

1) God's righteousness & praise Him 2) words of wisdom 3) praise of God 4) God's righteousness 5) wisdom & justice 6) nourishment to others 7) wisdom & fitting 8) psalms, hymns, spiritual songs.

Related scriptures: Ephesians 5:19; Psalm 37:30-31; Proverbs 10:20-21, 31-32.

Let your speech always be with grace, seasoned with salt, that you may know how you ought to answer each one.

—Colossians 4:6 NKJV

The Heart-Mouth Connection

The key to taming our tongue is in harnessing what's in our heart. Jesus said, "For a man's *heart* determines his *speech*. A good man's speech reveals the rich treasures within him. An evil-hearted man is filled with venom, and his speech reveals it" (Matthew 12:34-35 TLB, emphasis added). This heart-mouth connection runs throughout Scripture. Proverbs 16:23 declares, "A wise man's *heart* guides his *mouth*, and his lips promote instruction" (NIV, emphasis added). This is probably why David prayed, "May the words of my *mouth* and the meditation of my *heart* be pleasing to you, O Lord, my rock and my redeemer" (Psalm 19:14 NLT, emphasis added).

What do Proverbs 3:3, 7:3, and 2 Corinthians 3:3 all compare the *heart* to?

a tablet to be written on

What does the psalmist compare the *tongue* to in Psalm 45:1?

pen

What do these four verses taken together say to you about getting God's Word in your heart?

speak it w/ your "pen"

The best thing we can put in our heart is the Word of God. As we learned in chapter 6, there is no greater book on the face of the earth that holds the life-giving power of Scripture. It is the Word hidden in your heart that keeps you from sinning, lights your path, and guides you in the right direction.[10] With our heart we *receive* and *believe* the truth, and with our mouth we *confess* and *release* its saving power. If the Word of God is in your heart, it can be easily accessed by the Spirit and brought to your mouth.[11]

> ### Declaring HIS GREATNESS
>
> "The body of Christ must begin to live in the authority of the Word. For God's Word is creative power. ... The Word of God conceived in the heart, formed by the tongue, and spoken out of the mouth is creative power."
>
> —*Charles Capps*[9]

In what ways are you hiding God's Word in your heart? What evidence in your life confirms this?

___

___

> *Let the word of Christ **dwell in you richly** in all wisdom, teaching and admonishing one another in psalms and hymns and spiritual songs, singing with grace in your hearts to the Lord.*
>
> —Colossians 3:16 NKJV
> [emphasis added]

The Word of God is alive and full of power![12] It is God's supernatural strength working in our spirit, soul, and body to bring us salvation.[13] And we who have God's Word are instructed to *speak* His Word faithfully.[14] <u>The Word conceived in our heart, formed by the tongue, and spoken out of our mouth releases God's creative power. It will accomplish and achieve its purpose!</u>[15]

Read the account of *Jesus and the fig tree* in Mark 11:12-14, 20-24. What is the Holy Spirit showing you through this example about speaking DEATH to things that are not bearing good fruit? How does this apply to your life?

R - It's convicting in that I'm not producing any fruit

N - You can kill w/ words - I've been "killing" my marriage

Think About It

Why would Jesus curse a fig tree? Cultivated from the earliest times, figs grew on short, wide-spreading trees. Although figs are sometimes dried and made into cakes, they are ready to eat from the tree. In order to understand the account of Jesus and the fig tree, it is important to note that figs appear on the tree **before** the leaves emerge. If the leaves came out and no fruit appeared with them, the tree would remain barren for the entire season.[16]

Scripture says that Jesus was hungry. When He saw the fig tree in the distance that was full of leaves, He probably thought there would be figs ready to eat. But the tree lied to Him. Having leaves, it boasted of having fruit. But it didn't. It was a fake. *Lord, help us to be real and bear the fruit of Your Spirit—life-giving food to nourish others who are hungry for You...in Jesus' name.*

From Glory to Glory | 141

Read the account of *Ezekiel and the valley of bones* in Ezekiel 37:1-10. What is the Holy Spirit showing you through this example about speaking LIFE to things that seem dead (or impossible)? How does this apply to your life?

R - all things are possible; the same thing is possible in my life - I'm still salvageable.
W - I can speak life into my marriage

Remember, negative words nullify God's life-transforming power in your mouth. Ask Him for His grace to keep every trace of gossip, slander, lying, and complaining far from your lips.[17] As you hide His Word in your heart, it will flow from your mouth, bringing life and healing to all who hear.[18]

Prayer of praise
> Lord, thank you for loving me and allowing me to share in Your glory. Please forgive me for disobeying You in any way and for murmuring and complaining at times in the past. Remove any veil of deception from my heart. Keep me tender and responsive to Your touch. Help me to hide Your Word in my heart and speak it over my life. I want to see You do great things in me and through me. Thank you for the priceless gift of Your Holy Spirit and for having my best interest in mind at all times. You are truly amazing…in Jesus' name, amen.

My Journal
THINGS I WANT TO REMEMBER

> "We who fear God are continually being conformed into His image until we shine as brilliant lights in a dark world. This describes the awesome glory His faithful church shall emit in these last days. Glory to God forever!"
>
> **JOHN BEVERE**

God's Spirit is changing you into His image from one degree of glory to another. Open your heart to His Word and the wonderful work of His Spirit. As you choose to live a life of obedience, yielding your will to His and being a doer of

His Word, great things will take place. Take a few moments to sit quietly before the Lord and hear His heart. Write down any insights or instructions He gives to you.

_____
_____
_____
_____
_____
_____
_____
_____
_____
_____
_____
_____
_____

CHAPTER OVERVIEW

Before the foundation of the world, God planned for you to be transformed into His image and share His glory. This transformation is a *process* brought about through the fear of the Lord. While murmuring, complaining, and other forms of negativity stop the process, diligently seeking God, remaining attentive to His Word, and obeying what He reveals keep the transformation process going. In this state, the eyes of your heart remain clear and unveiled, enabling you to not only recognize His glory, but also be changed by it!

(1) John Bevere, *The Fear of the Lord* (Lake Mary, FL: Charisma House, A Strang Company, 1997, 2006) pp. 138-139. (2) Christian Quotes on *Contentment* (http://dailychristianquote.com/dcqcontent.html, retrieved 10/13/10). (3) See note 1, p. 145. (4) *Standing Firm: 365 Devotionals to Strengthen Your Faith*, compiled by Patti M. Hummel (St. San Luis Obispo, CA: Parable) p. 339. (5) Adapted from *Merriam-Webster's Desk Dictionary* (Springfield, MA: Merriam-Webster, Incorporated, 1995). (6) Adapted from *Noah Webster's First Edition of an American Dictionary of the English Language* (1828), Republished in facsimile edition by Foundation for American Christian Education (San Francisco, CA, 2000). (7) Christian quotes on *Change in Circumstances/Change in Character* (http://dailychristianquote.com/dcqchange.html, retrieved 10/13/10). (8) Joyce Meyer, *Enjoying Where You Are On the Way to Where You Are Going* (Tulsa, OK: Harrison House, Inc., 1996) pp. 200-201. (9) Charles Capps, *God's Creative Power Will Work for You* (Tulsa, OK: Harrison House, Inc., 1976) pp. 8, 15. (10) See Psalm 119:11, 105. (11) See Romans 10:8-10. (12) See Hebrews 4:12. (13) See Romans 1:16. (14) See Jeremiah 23:28. (15) See Isaiah 55:10-11. (16) Adapted from *Nelson's Illustrated Encyclopedia of Bible Facts*; James I. Packer, Merrill C. Tenney, William White, Jr. Editors (Nashville, TN: Thomas Nelson Publishers, 1995) p. 260. (17) See Titus 3:2; 1 Peter 2:1; 3:10-11. (18) See Proverbs 12:18; 15:4; 10:20-21, 31-32.

Deut. 5:31   It would have been better for us... = no fear of God

Blinded to God's glory by:

My Notes

serve God for who He is
vs
for what He can do

- immorality
- idol
- tempt L
- complain = symptom of lack of fear of God

tremble @ His word = obey God even if it hurts, to completion, even if don't see benefit

bondservant - give self into servitude - out of choice, not like slave

religious spirit = uses my Word to execute his own will.

veil = deception

James 1:25
obed. to God keeps your eyes uncovered

I can do all things thru Christ Who Strengthens me

Prov 3:5-6, 7-8

~~rebellion~~ partial obedience to God = rebellion

Ps 55:19 do not change cause do not fear God

*Friendship with the Lord is
reserved for those who fear him.
With them he shares
the secrets of his covenant.*

—Psalm 25:14 NLT
[emphasis added]

INTIMATE FRIENDSHIP

Please refer to session 8 of the teaching series, along with chapters 12, 13 and 14 in *The Fear of the Lord* book.

> "The fear of the Lord is the beginning, or starting place, of an intimate relationship with God. I believe this is the most exciting facet of walking in the fear of the Lord! It is the heart's desire of every true believer. It is the only thing that will ever bring lasting fulfillment."
>
> JOHN BEVERE

1 As we have learned, God is deeply in love with us! From the beginning, His desire has been to have an intimate relationship with all of mankind. Through Adam's sin, intimacy with God was greatly diminished. Through Jesus' sacrifice, it was fully restored.

a. When you hear the word *intimacy*, what positive things come to mind?

N- closeness, belonging, acceptance

b. What is the difference between knowing *about* God and knowing Him intimately?

a closer relationship; head knowledge vs heart knowledge

> **INTIMATE**
> "Near, close in friendship or acquaintance; a familiar friend or associate with whom the thoughts of another are entrusted without reserve; to share together."[1] Other synonyms for *intimate* include personal, cherished, warm, friendly, confidential, secret.

The Lord takes pleasure in those who fear Him,
in those who hope in His mercy.

—Psalm 147:11 NKJV

G 2 In order to better understand intimate friendship with the Lord, think about the relationship you have with your closest, dearest friend.

a. What things do you *share together* that make your relationship so enjoyable—why do you like being around him or her?
R - similiar interests; nonjudgmental in talking
N - things you can't/don't share w/ anyone else; there's total acceptance

b. What things do you do in order to stay connected in relationship and not drift apart?
R - it's up to the other person to stay connected w/ me
N - do activities together

c. What parallels can you draw from your answers to your relationship with the Lord?
R - similiar interests

G **3** Nothing on earth compares to being in a personal relationship with our heavenly Father. His presence is so sweet, so liberating, and so empowering! David was so right when he said, "Taste and see that the Lord is good. Oh, the joys of those who take refuge in him!" (Psalm 34:8 NLT).

> ### Declaring
> # HIS GREATNESS
> "Avail yourself of the greatest privilege this side of heaven. Jesus Christ died to make this communion and communication with the Father possible."
> —*Billy Graham*[2]

a. *a*What does God promise in James 4:8 about drawing near Him? *b*Who is to make the first move?

a. come near to God & He will come near to you

b. You are

b. God never wants you to be afraid to come to Him. Read Hebrews 4:15-16 and 10:19-22 and explain *why* you have access to His presence and *how* He wants you to enter.

why - thru J blood sacrifice

how - w/ confidence

Related scripture: Ephesians 3:12.

c. Describe what a more intimate relationship with the Lord would look like for you.

R -

N - "hear" His voice, feel His presence, talk w/ back & forth Him daily

> "The proof of Abraham's godly fear and faith was his *obedience*. To fear God is to *believe* God. To believe God is to *obey* Him. James pointed out that Abraham's obedience, fueled by His holy fear of God, resulted in *friendship* with God."
> ### JOHN BEVERE

[G] 4. What does God look for in a friend? In Scripture, He has given us many good examples from whom to learn. One person He repeatedly referred to as His friend was Abraham[3]—a man whose actions illustrate what it means to fear God.

   a. Everywhere Abraham went he built an altar to God. Think about it... What was the purpose of the altar? What does this signify about his character and devotion to God?

   1. Worship thru sacrifice 2. Every place he went he had a physical reminder of his devotion + need for the presence of God

   Related scriptures: Genesis 12:6-8; 13:4, 18.

   b. The biggest test of Abraham's life was when God asked him to sacrifice his son Isaac. Read the account in Genesis 22:1-19 and explain how his actions demonstrate his fear of God.

   totally obedient. He feared God more than the act of killing his son!

   c. How does Abraham's example encourage you? How does it challenge you?

   1 God will always come through

   2 I need to trust God more.

> *The fear of the Lord is a fountain of life,*
> *turning a man from the snares of death.*
>
> —Proverbs 14:27 NIV
> [emphasis added]

5. The test of whether or not we're walking in the fear of the Lord is determined by what we do in the *absence* of His manifest presence. In other words, do we proclaim God's faithfulness even when we haven't seen a trace of it for quite some time? Joseph did. And as a result, his family and an entire nation were saved from famine.

a. When times are tough and it seems like God is absent, how do you tend to act? How can you grow in this area?

R 1. impatient, questioning, sitting on my hands waiting

N 1. impatient, questioning, busywork
2. trust, pray, ask for wisdom, guidance

Don't think you're alone; we all have room to grow in this. The next time the pressure is on, pray and ask God for abundant grace to pass the test! (See James 4:6; 2 Corinthians 12:9.)

b. Through the power of the fear of the Lord, Joseph escaped the snares of jealousy, offense, anger, revenge, and adultery. How has fearing God kept *you* from deadly snares? What have you learned as a result?

R -

N - kept me from divorcing Rick - God can bring good out of bad situations

c. What does the Lord promise those who fear Him in the midst of adversity?

1) to be near, fulfills desires, hears & saves
2) sees & hears cries, delivers from all trouble; close to broken hearted, saves crushed in spirit,
3) snare if don't fear him

Check out Psalm 145:18-19; 34:11-22; Isaiah 8:11-14.

> ## Declaring
> # HIS GREATNESS
>
> "He has held me when I have had no more strength and have wondered how I would ever make it. He has held me when I have felt defeated by all that I had to do. When I have run to my El Shaddai, I have never come away wanting. He is my all-sufficient One. O Beloved, do you understand? Have you experienced Him as your El Shaddai? If not, He is waiting—arms opened wide—for you."
>
> —Kay Arthur[4]

G 6. Paul had much to say about the state of the church in the last days. As a devoted friend of God, he received unparalleled understanding of Scripture and prophetic insight from the Holy Spirit about what was to come before Christ's return, including a great falling away.

a. Why did Paul so urgently charge Timothy to *preach the Word*?[5] What happens in our lives when the Word is preached?

1 To thoroughly equip people for every good work

2 faith comes

Consider 2 Timothy 3:16-17 and Romans 10:17.

b. How do you think fearing the Lord will help you not depart from your faith in Christ?

If you fear God, you'll obey Him

It is the truth.

Consider Paul's instruction to Timothy in 2 Timothy 3:14-4:5 and Jeremiah 32:38-40.

c. Why do you think a lack of godly fear will cause many to abandon their faith?

They'll respond more to what they do fear - man.

Consider 2 Timothy 3:1-5; 4:3-4 and 1 Timothy 4:1-2.

> "Paul said the only way to present people perfect in Christ is not only to *teach* them but to *warn* them as well (see Colossians 1:28). As a boy, my father's teachings helped me in life. But his warnings *saved* my life. When I ran out into the street to get a ball and my father screamed, 'Johnny!' I froze. His voice was so stern. But his warnings saved my life."
>
> JOHN BEVERE

7. In the times in which we live, seeing things clearly is very important. <u>By fearing the Lord, we can see things the way God sees them.</u> However, without the fear of the Lord, our discernment will be impaired.

Meditate on Jesus' words in Matthew 6:22-23
The lamp of the body is the eye. If therefore your eye is good, your whole body will be full of light. But if your eye is bad, your whole body will be full of darkness. If therefore the light that is in you is darkness, how great is that darkness!

NKJV

• • • • • •

The eye is the lamp of the body. So if your eye is sound, your entire body will be full of light. But if your eye is unsound, your whole body will be full of darkness. If then the very light in you [your conscience] is darkened, how dense is that darkness!

AMP

a. What causes our eyes to be darkened? What makes them clear and sound? What is the Holy Spirit speaking to you from this passage?

dark - sin

clear - truth obeying the

b. How do you think Paul's prayer in Ephesians relates to Jesus' words? What does it say to you personally?

I keep asking that the God of our Lord Jesus Christ, the glorious Father, may give you the Spirit of wisdom and revelation, so that you may know him better. I pray also that the eyes of your heart may be enlightened in order that you may know the hope to which he has called you, the riches of his glorious inheritance in the saints, and his incomparably great power for us who believe.

—*Ephesians 1:17-19* NIV

> *Surely the Sovereign Lord does nothing without revealing his plan to his servants the prophets.*
>
> —Amos 3:7 NIV

> *Friendship with the Lord is reserved for those who fear him. With them he shares the secrets of his covenant.*
>
> —Psalm 25:14 NLT

8. One of the most amazing blessings of walking in the fear of the Lord and being His friend is that He often chooses to share His intentions and future plans with us—*before* they take place. For example…

   a. Noah found favor in God's eyes, and as a result, God showed him His plan to destroy the earth and mankind by water. How did this insight help Noah and direct his actions?

      He believed what God said & built the ark

      Check out Genesis 6:5-22.

   b. God revealed to Abraham His plan to destroy Sodom and Gomorrah because of their wickedness. How did this knowledge motivate Abraham and direct his actions?

      He interceded

      Check out Genesis 18:17-33 (especially verses 22-33).

   c. From these examples, what are some reasons for God revealing His future plans to us, His friends? How does this encourage and challenge you?

      to prepare & to warn

Intimate Friendship | 153

Think About It

A Tale of Two Believers
Abraham and Lot are both referred to in Scripture as righteous. However, when we take a closer look at each man's character, there are some major differences. While Abraham was not perfect, he was a man who feared the Lord, walked in obedience, sought peace with others, and was a generous worshipper of God. Lot, on the other hand, was a man of selfish ambition who put his interests above others' and kind of fit God in when it was convenient. While Abraham was *committed* to God, Lot was *carnal* and mesmerized by things of the world. Time after time, Lot got into trouble because he was at the wrong place at the wrong time with the wrong people. His life was a joke to others and in the end he fathered two tribes of people who became a major thorn in Israel's side. Had it not been for the prayers and intervention of Abraham, his life wouldn't have lasted as long as it did. **What's the moral of this tale?** Don't be like Lot, living a wasted life and being saved by the skin of your teeth. Follow the path that Abraham pioneered. Fear the Lord, put Him first in all you do, and your life will leave a legacy of blessing for generations to come!

Check out the story of Abraham's life in Genesis 12-25 and Lot's life in Genesis 13-14, and 19.

9. Make no mistake—when you fear the Lord, you have His attention. He is mindful of you at all times, and His blessings are on your life. Read this passage of promise in Malachi 3:16-18 (NLT):

Then those who feared the Lord spoke with each other, and the Lord listened to what they said. In his presence, a scroll of remembrance was written to record the names of those who feared him and always thought about the honor of his name.

"They will be my people," says the Lord of Heaven's Armies. "On the day when I act in judgment, they will be my own special treasure. I will spare them as a father spares an obedient child. Then you will again see the difference between the righteous and the wicked, between those who serve God and those who do not."

Related scriptures: Revelation 3:7-12; Luke 1:50; Psalm 31:19; 147:11.

How do these verses say your life will be blessed now and in eternity by fearing God?

goodness, unfailing love, mercy, crown, being kept from hour of trial

Declaring His Greatness

"Christ is like a river that is continually flowing. There are always fresh supplies of water coming from the fountain-head, so that a man may live by it and be supplied with water all his life. So Christ is an ever-flowing fountain; he is continually supplying his people, and the fountain is not spent. They who live upon Christ may have fresh supplies from him for all eternity; they may have an increase of blessedness that is new, and new still, and which never will come to an end."

—*Jonathan Edwards*[6]

10 Would you like the level of intimacy between you and God to *grow*? He would. He yearns to be personally involved in every part of your life. Not just on Sunday, but also Monday through Saturday—24/7.

a. What are you presently doing, or have done in the past, that enables you to tune out the world around you and really feel close to the Lord?

R - turn off TV

N - praise Him

b. What are you willing to exchange in order to have more quality time with the Lord?

R

N - TV

c. *Get quiet before the Lord.* Ask Him if there is anything He'd like you to change in your schedule, commitments, hobbies, etc., to draw closer to Him. Write what He reveals.

_____

_____

_____

> *All has been heard; the end of the matter is: Fear God [revere and worship Him, knowing that He is] and keep His commandments, for this is the whole of man [the full, original purpose of his creation, the object of God's providence, the root of character, the foundation of all happiness, the adjustment to all inharmonious circumstances and conditions under the sun] and the whole [duty] for every man.*
>
> —Ecclesiastes 12:13 AMP

The Blessings of Fearing God

And the Lord our God commanded us to obey all these decrees and to fear him so he can continue to bless us and preserve our lives, as he has done to this day.

—Deuteronomy 6:24 NLT

Where is the man who fears the Lord? God will teach him how to choose the best. He shall live within God's circle of blessing, and his children shall inherit the earth.

—Psalm 25:12-13 TLB

Fear of the Lord lengthens one's life, but the years of the wicked are cut short.

—Proverbs 10:27 NLT

Humility and the fear of the Lord bring wealth and honor and life.

—Proverbs 22:4 NIV

Right Where You Live
PUTTING IN A GOOD WORD

As iron sharpens iron, so a friend sharpens a friend.

—Proverbs 27:17 NLT

The power of true friends is incredible! Their encouragement can inspire us to soar to new heights and carry on when times are hard. Their constructive criticism can keep us from making devastating mistakes or rash decisions we will regret later on. Galatians 6:10 tells us that "...whenever we have the opportunity, we should do good to everyone—*especially to those in the family of faith*" (NLT, emphasis added). One way we can do good to our brothers and sisters in Christ is by taking time to point out their strengths. As we learned in the last chapter, words are powerful, and when used the right way, can release life.

Try this exercise of encouragement:
Ask each member of your group to take a sheet of paper and write their name at the top of it. Have them pass it around to the others. Each person is to write one positive quality about the other members of the group. This is a quality you admire and respect them for—something you see in them that builds up and encourages others. Once everyone has had a chance to share, each person's sheet should be returned to its rightful owner. If time allows, group members can verbally share what they wrote for each person.

Adjust the activity to fit your group
This activity can be done within a church group, amongst coworkers, between husband and wife, between family members (immediate and extended), etc. For smaller groups, you can increase the number of good qualities you write to five, ten, or more.

Write what you observe
Overall, how did the activity affect the members of your group?

_____
_____
_____
_____

How were you affected by everyone's comments? Did you learn anything new about yourself? Did you find anything hard to believe or receive?

___

Similar exercises have been conducted in schools and churches across the country for some time now. The impact on one man was so great that he kept the encouraging words of his fellow peers in his wallet for more than 30 years. Another person was so touched by the heartfelt statements of others that he decided not to take his life. *What other things can you do to sharpen the lives of those in your group?*

> ### Declaring
> ### HIS GREATNESS
>
> "The glory of friendship is not the outstretched hand, or the kindly smile, or the joy of companionship. It is the spiritual inspiration that comes to one when he discovers that someone else believes in him and is willing to trust him with his friendship."
>
> —*Corrie ten Boom*[7]

Weekly Devotional 8

HUMILITY—THE ESSENCE OF FEARING GOD

The fear of the Lord teaches a man wisdom, and humility comes before honor. Humility and the fear of the Lord bring wealth and honor and life.

—Proverbs 15:33; 22:4 NIV

The doorway to intimate friendship with God is having the fear of the Lord, and the key to walking in the fear of the Lord is a heart of *humility*. These two expressions of God's Spirit work hand in hand. If we could get a spiritual microscope and place a sample of the fear of the Lord under its magnifying eye, we would see humility woven into the fibers of its structure. Think about it... By definition, *humility* is "freedom from pride and arrogance; humbleness of mind; a deep sense of unworthiness in the sight of God, and submission to the divine will."[8]

If there was ever a person who had an understanding of humility, it was **Andrew Murray**. His life's theme was the "casting of self" upon Christ.[9] This man of God ministered for more than 60 years and wrote more than 200 books. Notice how he defines humility:

> "**Humility**, the place of entire dependence on God, is, from the very nature of things, the first duty and the highest virtue of the creature. In fact, *it is the root of every virtue.* And so *pride,* or the loss of this humility, is the root of every sin and evil!
>
> Humility is the only soil in which the graces root; the lack of humility is the sufficient explanation of every defect and failure. Humility is not so much a grace or virtue along with others as it is the root of all, because *it alone takes the right attitude before God* and allows Him as God to do all."[10]

Jesus Christ embodied this "right attitude" of both true humility and the fear of the Lord. This is most clearly seen throughout the Gospel of John where He repeatedly points out that He did not say or do anything of His own will; He only did what the Father instructed Him.[11] He did not have His own agenda. He did not seek to build His own kingdom. His only desire was to please the Father and bring Him glory. Indeed, He *delighted* in the fear of the Lord (see Isaiah 11:3).

The opposite of humility is pride. It is the original sin found within Lucifer that got him kicked out of heaven and is probably the biggest obstacle to living and growing in the fear of the Lord. A proud heart exalts self and does not want to reverence, honor, or fear the Lord. It truly is the root of all sin. Andrew Murray continues…

> "Evil can have no beginning but from pride and no end but from humility. The truth is this: Pride must die in you or nothing of heaven can live in you. Under the banner of the truth, give yourself up to the meek and humble spirit of the holy Jesus."[12]

The deceitfulness of pride within us dupes us to believe that we have power, wisdom, and goodness *apart* from God. Nothing could be further from the truth. Apart from Him, we can do nothing (see John 15:5).

Meditate on the Message
It is the Spirit Who gives life [He is the Life-giver]; the flesh conveys no benefit whatever [there is no profit in it]. The words (truths) that I have been speaking to you are spirit and life.

—*John 6:63* AMP

For I know that nothing good dwells within me, that is, in my flesh. I can will what is right, but I cannot perform it. [I have the intention and urge to do what is right, but no power to carry it out.]
—*Romans 7:18* AMP

For it is we who are the circumcision, we who worship by the Spirit of God, who glory in Christ Jesus, and who put no confidence in the flesh.
—*Philippians 3:3* NIV

What do these verses say to you about your *flesh*? On what should your attention be focused? Why?

_____
_____
_____

Meditate on the Message
All who *fear the Lord* will hate evil. Therefore, I hate *pride* and arrogance, corruption and perverse speech.
—*Proverbs 8:13* NLT

In his pride the wicked does not seek him; in all his thoughts *there is no room for God.*
—*Psalm 10:4* NIV

Pride leads to disgrace, but with *humility* comes *wisdom*.
—*Proverbs 11:2* NLT

Pride goes before destruction, and a haughty spirit before a fall.
—*Proverbs 16:18* NKJV

A man's pride will bring him low, but the *humble* in spirit will retain *honor*.
—*Proverbs 29:23* NKJV
[emphasis added]

How do you think pride prevents us from having the fear of the Lord? How does humility promote it?

_____
_____

According to James 4:6-7 and 1 Peter 5:5-6, what is the connection between having a *humble heart* and receiving God's *grace* (power and ability) to live a victorious, godly life?

_____

_____

_____

Related scriptures: Proverbs 3:34; 15:25.

Humility and the fear of the Lord come from the same source
Where does humility come from? It cannot be purchased at a Christian conference or developed through college training. It can only be received from Christ Himself. He *is* humility. Clearly, it is only through the supernatural work of His Spirit, dwelling in our spirits, that we receive humility. The same is true of the fear of the Lord; this virtue cannot be taught by man. It must be infused and cultivated in our spirit by God's Spirit. Andrew Murray continues…

> "Humility is not a thing that will come of itself, but that it must be made the object of special desire and prayer and faith and practice. …Let us study the character of Christ until our souls are filled with the love and admiration of His lowliness. And let us believe that, when we are broken down under a sense of our pride, and of our impotence to cast it out, Jesus Christ Himself will come in to impart this grace too as a part of His wondrous life within us."[13]

Jesus gives you a special invitation to draw near to Him in an intimate relationship. Read His encouraging and empowering words:

Come to Me, all you who labor and are heavy-laden and overburdened, and I will cause you to rest. [I will ease and relieve and refresh your souls.]

Take My yoke upon you and learn of Me, for I am gentle (meek) and humble (lowly) in heart, and you will find rest (relief and ease and refreshment and recreation and blessed quiet) for your souls.

For My yoke is wholesome (useful, good--not harsh, hard, sharp, or pressing, but comfortable, gracious, and pleasant), and My burden is light and easy to be borne.

—*Matthew 11:28-30* AMP

What is the Holy Spirit speaking to you through this passage? Will you accept Jesus' invitation?

There is one more key element that opens our hearts and prepares us to receive the precious gifts of humility and the fear of the Lord, and that is *prayer*. Put simply, prayer is talking to and listening to God. It is communication and communion—a two-way dialogue between us and the Father. What an amazing privilege! Prayer is not an occasional event but an ongoing lifestyle. We are repeatedly encouraged throughout Scripture to pray continually with all types of prayer.[15]

> ### Declaring His Greatness
>
> "A *humble* heart is like a magnet that *draws the favor of God* toward us."
> —*Jim Cymbala*[14]

That being said, how do you think *prayer, humility,* and *the fear of the Lord* work together to help you enjoy an ongoing, intimate relationship with God?

Consider: Jeremiah 29:12-13; Proverbs 3:5-8; Psalm 25:9; 2 Chronicles 7:14-16; Isaiah 57:15.

Friend of God, may He grant you the humility of Christ and His holy reverential fear to experience the full life He has planned for you!

Prayer for humility

O Lord, please grant me the humility of Christ. His humble heart and His reverential fear of You opened the door to the deepest, most intimate friendship anyone on earth has ever had. I want that kind of relationship with You! Forgive me for being proud. Take every trace of pride from my heart. Help me be mindful to clothe myself with humility daily so that I can stay intimately connected with You. You are awesome, Lord! From this day through eternity, I look forward to a growing friendship with You that is beyond my wildest dreams...in Jesus' name, amen.

My Journal
THINGS I WANT TO REMEMBER

> "I believe with all my heart that this generation will be the greatest generation that has ever walked the face of the earth. ...I believe that we will be the great generation that the prophets wrote about—where sons and daughters, menservants and maidservants are prophesying the Word of the Lord and nations are coming into His kingdom. May God help us to return to the fear of the Lord so that we can fulfill our destiny!"
>
> JOHN BEVERE

Have you enjoyed this study on the fear of the Lord? Has it opened your eyes to new things about God? Has it given you a hunger to draw closer to Him? Take a few moments to offer Him thanks and praise for what He has taught you. He is worthy of our worship! What a privilege we have to be in relationship with Him. Write down any new insights or direction He is revealing.

_____

_____

_____

_____

CHAPTER OVERVIEW
The most exciting and rewarding blessing of fearing the Lord is the privilege of being in an intimate relationship with Him. Friendship is reserved for those who fear Him. Nothing on earth compares with this liberating and empowering connection. God confides in those who fear Him, sharing the secrets of His covenant and the intentions of His future plans. Through humility and the fear of the Lord, your life will be strengthened with endurance and blessed beyond measure both now and through eternity!

---

(1) Adapted from *Noah Webster's First Edition of an American Dictionary of the English Language* (1828), Republished in facsimile edition by Foundation for American Christian Education (San Francisco, CA, 2000). (2) Quotes by *Billy Graham* (http://dailychristianquote.com/dcqgraham.html, retrieved 10-8-10). (3) See 2 Chronicles 20:7; Isaiah 41:8; James 2:23. (4) Quotes on *Comfort* (http://dailychristianquote.com/dcqcomfort.html, retrieved 10/20/10). (5) See 2 Timothy 4:1-2. (6) *Fast Break: Five-Minute Devotions to Start Your Day* (St. San Luis Obispo, CA: Parable, 2007) Day 238. (7) Ibid, Day 278. (8) See note 1. (9) Adapted from *131 Christians Everyone Should Know*, Andrew Murray (www.christianitytoday.com/history/special/131christians/murray.html, retrieved 9/22/07). (10) Andrew Murray, *Humility* (Fort Washington, PA: CLC Publications, 2006) pp. 12, 14. (11) See John 5:30; 6:38; 7:16; 8:28, 42, 50; 14:10, 24. (12) See note 10, p. 101. (13) Ibid, pp. 15-16. (14) See note 6, Day 314. (15) See 1 Thessalonians 5:17; Luke 18:1; Ephesians 6:18; Matthew 7:7-11.

My Notes

Obedience keeps veil off - can understand
Phil 2:12-13

God reserves ~~Ps 25:14~~ friendship & secrets w/ those who fear Him.

The Fear of the Lord

UNLOCK GOD'S TREASURES IN YOUR LIFE...
What is the fear of the Lord? What does it look like? John Bevere reveals from Scripture this often-overlooked and misunderstood life-saving truth. It is the key to wisdom, knowledge, and intimacy with God.

You will be challenged throughout this powerful curriculum to embrace the fear of the Lord in your daily life. If you are ready to grow in your knowledge of God, then this study is for you. Whether used individually or in a group, this riveting message will revolutionize your life!

CURRICULUM INCLUDES:
- 8 VIDEO SESSIONS ON 3 DVDs (30 MINUTES EACH)
- 8 AUDIO SESSIONS ON 4 CDs (30 MINUTES EACH)
- THE FEAR OF THE LORD BOOK
- DEVOTIONAL WORKBOOK
- PROMOTIONAL MATERIAL TO HELP GATHER GROUPS

Churches & Pastors –
Local churches are the passion and heart of this ministry. Our Church Relations team connects with pastors, churches and ministry leaders worldwide. It is their joy and honor to encourage leaders, pray for churches, provide life-transforming resources, and build authentic relationships.

UNITED STATES	**AUSTRALIA**	**UNITED KINGDOM**
1-800-648-1477	1-300-650-577	0800-9808-933

JOIN OVER 300,000 PEOPLE WHOSE LIVES HAVE BEEN TRANSFORMED BY OUR CURRICULUMS.

Extraordinary
CURRICULUM

The *Extraordinary* Curriculum is an extensive journey with 12 video and audio sessions, a thought-provoking devotional workbook, and a hardcover book. As each session builds, you will be positioned to step into the unknown and embrace your divine empowerment.

INCLUDES:
- 12 30-MINUTE VIDEO SESSIONS ON 4 DVDS
- 12 30-MINUTE AUDIO SESSIONS ON 6 CDS
- HARDCOVER BOOK
- DEVOTIONAL WORKBOOK
- PROMOTIONAL MATERIALS

BREAKING INTIMIDATION
CURRICULUM

Everyone has been intimidated at some point in life. Do you really know why it happened or how to keep it from happening again? John Bevere exposes the root of intimidation, challenges you to break its fearful grip, and teaches you to release God's gifts and establish His dominion in your life.

INCLUDES:
- EIGHT 30-MINUTE VIDEO SESSIONS ON 3 DVDS
- EIGHT 30-MINUTE AUDIO SESSIONS ON 4 CDS
- BREAKING INTIMIDATION BOOK
- DEVOTIONAL WORKBOOK
- PROMOTIONAL MATERIALS

HONOR'S REWARD
CURRICULUM

This curriculum will unveil the power and truth of an often overlooked principle–Honor. If you understand the vital role of this virtue, you will attract blessing both now and for eternity. This insightful message teaches you how to extend honor to your Creator, family members, authorities and those who surround your world.

INCLUDES:
- 12 30-MINUTE VIDEO LESSONS ON 4 DVDS
- 12 30-MINUTE AUDIO LESSONS ON 6 CDS
- HONOR'S REWARD HARDCOVER BOOK
- DEVOTIONAL WORKBOOK
- PROMOTIONAL MATERIALS

DRIVEN by Eternity
CURRICULUM
Making Your Life Count Today & Forever

We were made for eternity. This life on earth is but a vapor. Yet too many live as though there is nothing on the other side. Scriptural laws and principles may be applied to achieve success on earth, but are we prepared for eternity? This power-packed teaching, including an allegory on the Kingdom of Affabel, will help you understand that the choices you make today will determine how you spend eternity.

INCLUDES:
- 12 40-MINUTE VIDEO LESSONS ON 4 DVDS
- DRIVEN BY ETERNITY HARDCOVER BOOK
- HARDCOVER DEVOTIONAL WORKBOOK
- AFFABEL AUDIO THEATER

THE BAIT OF SATAN
CURRICULUM

Jesus said, "It's impossible that no offenses will come."
–Luke 17:1

A most crucial message for believers in this hour.

"This message is possibly the most important confrontation with truth you'll encounter in your lifetime. The issue of offense – the very core of *The Bait of Satan* – is often the most difficult obstacle an individual must face and overcome."

– John Bevere

INCLUDES:
- 12 30-MINUTE VIDEO LESSONS ON 4 DVDs
- 12 30-MINUTE AUDIO LESSONS ON 6 CDs
- BEST-SELLING BOOK THE BAIT OF SATAN
- DEVOTIONAL WORKBOOK
- PROMOTIONAL MATERIALS

A HEART ABLAZE
CURRICULUM

Jesus has never accepted lukewarmness. Rather, He calls for passion! This message will challenge you to exchange a mediocre relationship with God for a vibrant, fiery one.

INCLUDES:
- 12 30-MINUTE VIDEO LESSONS ON 4 DVDs
- 12 30-MINUTE AUDIO LESSONS ON 6 CDs
- A HEART ABLAZE best-selling book
- DEVOTIONAL WORKBOOK
- PROMOTIONAL MATERIALS

UNDER COVER
CURRICULUM

Under the shadow of the Almighty, there is liberty, provision and protection. Unfortunately, many don't understand how to find this secret place. In this curriculum you will learn how biblical submission differs from obedience. You will also learn the distinction between direct and delegated authority and how to respond to and overcome unfair treatment.

INCLUDES:
- 12 30-MINUTE VIDEO LESSONS ON 4 DVDs
- 12 30-MINUTE AUDIO LESSONS ON 6 CDs
- BEST-SELLING BOOK UNDER COVER
- DEVOTIONAL WORKBOOK
- PROMOTIONAL MATERIALS

DRAWING NEAR
CURRICULUM

Drawing extensively from his own journey, John has specially written and prepared this *Drawing Near* message to lead you into times of private and intimate communion with God Himself. This devotional kit acts as a treasure map, guiding you around potential pitfalls and breaking through personal barriers leading you into new and glorious realms of a lifelong adventure with God!

INCLUDES:
- 12 30-MINUTE VIDEO LESSONS ON 4 DVDs
- BEST-SELLING BOOK DRAWING NEAR
- 84-DAY DEVOTIONAL
- WORKBOOK